African American Voices: African American Health Educators Speak Out

African American Voices: African American Health Educators Speak Out

Ruth W. Johnson
Editor

National League for Nursing Press • New York
Pub. No. 14-2631

ISBN 0-88737-625-8

The views expressed in this publication represent the views of the authors and does not necessarily reflect the official views of the National League for Nursing.

This book was set in Galliard by Publications Development Company. The editor and designer was Allan Graubard. The cover was designed by Lauren Stevens.

Printed in the United States of America

*C*ontents

Contents

*C*ontributors

Sonia Baker, PhD, RN, CNA, Aaron Diamond Post-Doctoral Research Fellow, Columbia University School of Public Health, New York, NY

Antoinette A. Coleman, PhD, LCSW, ACSW, Norfolk State University School of Social Work, Norfolk, VA

Agnes M. Richardson-Collins, MSN, RN, Norfolk State University Department of Nursing, Norfolk, VA

Bertha L. Davis, PhD, RN, FAAN, Dean, Hampton University School of Nursing, Hampton, VA

Pamela V. Hammond, PhD, RN, Hampton University School of Nursing, Hampton, VA

Ruth W. Johnson, EdD, RN, FAAN, Campus Director, College of New Rochelle, School of New Resources. Former Director of Council Affairs, Council of Baccalaureate & Higher Degree Programs, National League for Nursing.

Delroy M. Louden, PhD, Vice President, Division of Research, National League for Nursing. Dr. Louden is currently a recipient of a Public Health Service Primary Care Policy Fellowship.

Sandra Millon-Underwood, PhD, RN, University of Wisconsin–Milwaukee School of Nursing and UWM–House of Peace Nursing Center Director, Milwaukee, WI

Sandra Sayles-Cross, PhD, RN, University of Texas–Tyler, Tyler, TX

DeLois P. Weekes, DNSc, RN, Boston College School of Nursing, Boston, MA

*F*oreword

This book offers a potpourri of slices and selections from health care issues facing individuals, families, and communities of African descent in the nineties. With unerring precision, the authors expose possibly inherent high risk for illness related to one's racial identity. The risks described include cancer, kidney disease, physical and sexual abuse, chronic illness, teen pregnancy, stress, and schizophrenia. These are all human ailments, but the morbidity and mortality rates for some and the potential outcome of institutionalization for others are greater for those of African descent than for the general white population. For example, cancer in blacks kills more frequently than in whites and schizophrenia is more frequently diagnosed in young black males in emergency rooms than in white males.

With scholarly discipline the authors question whether the results are color related or due to variables such as socio-economic status or to the interaction of color and other variables. While there are no clear answers, this book offers an exploration and study of a variety of health care issues that challenge the strength of the family and community of African origin in a changing health care system.

These challenges include the implementation of strategies to more effectively access health delivery systems; the development of coping skills in the management of stress as care-receivers and care-givers; and the development of collaborative, community-based approaches to the prevention of violence within families and communities.

As we prepared this foreword, we questioned to whom the challenge should be given. Each reader, each student, each practitioner, each researcher, and each educator must respond to the challenge. This response must begin with an understanding of the issues and a willingness to begin a journey to appreciate differences as well as a commitment to change one's self as well as one's community. This book represents a place of beginning. . . .

Janice G. Brewington,
PhD, RN, FAAN
Asst. Dean and Associate Professor
North Carolina Agriculture &
State University

Beverly Malone,
PhD, RN, FAAN
Dean and Professor
North Carolina Agriculture
& State University

Introduction

Ruth W. Johnson

When I was first approached about writing a book on the issues related to health and health care in the African American community, I was thrilled. For the first time in recent history, the League was reaching out to African American nurse educators who, for the most part, have found it difficult to publish about health issues in their communities. I immediately asked, why just one book? The issues are diverse and the situations drastic. Why not a series of books where major ethnic nurse educators would have an opportunity to write a chapter or edit a volume? Health interventions themselves admit a great diversity, and here is a direct means to reach educators, clinicians, and students. Indeed, here is a means to discuss, critique, challenge, and hopefully advance our understanding of health and health care for African Americans and all other minority groups. The idea, I am glad to say, was quickly accepted and the effort begun with this first collection.

I then set out to identify nurse educators from across the country who, while making significant contributions to the African American community, had not yet had national exposure. I based my decision to use a cross-sectional approach in the selection of contributing authors on several factors. First, I wanted to give the reader a perspective on African American life in the United States much broader than that expressed by the tiresome phrase "ghetto life," which too many European-American nurse educators associate all too quickly with African American life as a whole. Second, the health issues confronting African American communities throughout the country are as much local as they are regional in nature. As such, any health care strategies brought to bear must be appropriately local and informed of, even animated by, broader perspectives. Third, I desired to expose the African American nurse educators, as a group, to the population of readers associated with the National League for Nursing Press.

The African American nurse educators who agreed to participate in this project are known locally and regionally. They have demonstrated their knowledge, expertise, research ability, and competency, and have extended their knowledge beyond the formal context of the university. They are caring individuals with significant views on the health and health care of African American communities throughout the United States.

When I received the first set of manuscript, I knew that this endeavor was well on the way. Contributors had selected topics carefully and tried to avoid duplication. If several authors did select the same content area, we agreed to approach it from varying perspectives. For example, in the book you will read several chapters concerned with children. One chapter speaks of the abuse of children, another chapter addresses the health issues of adolescents. The majority of the chapters focus on adulthood and those issues pertinent to all developmental aspects of adult life. Significant as well is the inclusion of one chapter on cancer and one chapter on organ transplants in the African American community. These two chapters successfully reveal the unspoken but practicing cultural beliefs of some African Americans. They demonstrate African American beliefs about organ transplant and how some African Americans view illness, factors significant to the course and effect of illness and outcome. I believe these two chapters suggest the tremendous amount of work and education still to be performed by health care workers. I am not suggesting that we attempt to change the presiding culture here. Rather, I am suggesting that information and education occur so that African Americans can make health care choices based on a more appropriate understanding of facts regarding their particular health concerns. In addition, it seems to me that these two chapters provide some insight into the culture of what the majority community has often, and mistakenly, labeled as fatalism on the part of African Americans. Fatalism, we must remember, is only a symptom. It is not a cause and offers little, if any, basis for substantive health care interventions.

Consistent throughout each chapter is the identification of another major issue for African Americans: access to health care. For many African Americans in the United States, access to health services is not always possible. Nor do African Americans always obtain the care they need. African Americans who are in a higher socioeconomic group may find that health and health care is better for them. Nonetheless, for most African Americans this simply isn't true. It is shocking that the old issues of education and health identified over 20 years ago continue to plague contemporary America, and especially African Americans, as much or more so today. It is no longer adequate to ask why these problems exist. I believe that most fairly educated people know the answer. Racism and prejudice continue to thrive. Society continues to view and stereotype African Americans as a whole. That African Americans are as divergent as their European counterparts is, if admitted, rarely taken to heart.

As I read each chapter, however, I did not feel the euphoria I had anticipated and that the decision to begin the project had generated. Rather, each chapter poignantly suggested that the struggle continues for equity in all aspects of life, health, and health care. Initially, too, I wondered and marveled at the faculty who participated. I asked myself how, as nurse educators, they could write about the very pressing issues confronting African Americans without becoming more emotional, frustrated, even angry. How could a group of highly educated and sophisticated nurse educators write so matter of factly, even if scholarly, about situations that should have African American health care educators and practitioners pounding the doors of the establishment regarding health and health care of African Americans. Where is the outrage, the dissatisfaction, the hurt? These thoughts constantly and consistently troubled me. Then, too, I was embarrassed because I felt that somehow I was not being absolutely fair to my colleagues. Perhaps I was, in fact, too critical. Perhaps I was searching for positions that need not be present for advances to be made. Perhaps the very essence of being African American in this country, as I conceived it, had been lost. A sense of struggle for health care was dramatically absent. Why?

I pondered this question for some time and decided that any answer, or group of answers, were sufficient to spark another book. At the very least, they were cause for considerable discussion. For now, I will say simply that, in my experience, it is doubly difficult for minority nurse educators to openly write all they might think and feel. We have learned to present our work very carefully in a style and manner considered socially and professionally acceptable. Many minority nurse educators serve on faculties where they may very well be the only nurse educator of color. Survival and tenure as a faculty member could possibly require the toning and shaping of what they write, and especially about an author's own racial or ethnic group, into channels more formally accepted.

There are nurse educators who will question this statement or who may challenge my assertion as particularist or just not true. In response, I would pose this question: How many times have we heard of situations where an African American nurse educator or any African American faculty member was fired or terminated from their teaching position because they were too black or they spoke and focused too much on cultural diversity, or, as one faculty member recently told me, they made students and faculty members too uncomfortable? Are we truly free as educators to teach what we feel and know by our research as aspects of an evolving reality? And what are the consequences when and if we do? These questions are and need to be asked by each one of us as minority nurse educators. Or does survival as a minority nurse educator require our conformity in the service of assumed prerogatives? In effect, do we say and write what motivates us as members of our communities and our professions?

You, the reader, will be the judge. What do you think? Keep in mind the findings of the final chapter by Dr. Louden, an epidemiologist, whose study of Afro-Caribbean blacks living in England demonstrates the possible effects of a culturally alien environment on the diagnosis of mental illness, in this case, schizophrenia. Behaviors, life styles, values, morals, and ethics can be misinterpreted within socially dominant paradigms. For African American nurse educators and for all African American people, it is essential that we remain very clear not only about who we are, but where we are, and how we need to structure and organize ourselves to avoid victimization wherever we may encounter it. Finally, it is up to us, as it has always been, to obtain, develop, and enhance our health and our health care.

Chapter One

African Americans and Participation in Kidney Organ Donation: Selected Issues

Sonia Baker

In 1990, there were an estimated 210,000 people in the United States diagnosed with end stage renal disease (ESRD) (United States Renal Data System, 1993). ESRD is a life threatening illness. The etiology of ESRD has been well-documented and linked as a terminal phase from severe pre-conditions such as diabetes, hypertension, glomerulonephritis, cystic disease, other urologic diseases, other identifiable diseases, and causes unknown (United States Renal Data System).

Along racial lines, Caucasians and African Americans comprised 66 and 30 percent, respectively, of the total population of ESRD patients (United States Renal Data System, 1993). In looking at this estimate, the incidence of ESRD (30%) among African Americans is disturbing when compared to their estimated resident population (12%) in the United States (United States Bureau of Census, 1993).

Although primary prevention and early treatment is viewed as the preferred lines of defense against the destructive progression of diseases, many African Americans are either not aware or do not seek treatment in a timely manner. Numerous socioeconomic deficits such as inadequate access to health care in poor minority communities, insurance coverage, rising health care costs, noncompliance with prescribed medical protocol, and lack of knowledge about prevention and treatment are suggested factors related to African Americans for not receiving adequate health care and the subsequent development of terminal diseases (Livingston, 1993;

United States Renal Data System, 1993). Quite often, by the time African Americans enter the health care system for diagnosis or treatment, their pre-condition status has progressed to irreversible organ damage such as in the case of ESRD.

For ESRD patients, selected treatments may include dialysis; however, the treatment of choice is compatible kidney transplants. From receiving a successful transplant, the patient's quality of life is enhanced by having a functioning kidney which cleanses the system continuously, as opposed to intermittently by the dialysis procedure. Other benefits include the cost-effectiveness of a transplant procedure versus the long-term expenses that are incurred from continued dialysis treatments. In addition, most dialysis patients are unable to independently sustain themselves financially, while those receiving transplants are often able to return to work. From a social point of view, the patient can participate in activities without the need to plan around the dialysis schedule or adhere to the strict dietary requirements associated with dialysis. Finally, the self-esteem of the patient is elevated by knowing that their ability to live is not directly dependent on the operation of an external dialysis procedure (Evans, Bragg, & Bryan, 1981; Livingston, 1993; Prottas, 1983; United States Renal Data System, 1993).

Although the treatment of choice for ESRD patients are compatible kidney transplants, there is a gap in the supply and demand of available kidney donors particularly for African Americans. Multiple reasons for this gap include a shortage of available organs, donor-recipient incompatibility, prolonged waiting time, and the reluctance among African Americans to donate organs. In this chapter, then, I will discuss issues related to the problem of kidney procurement for African American recipients and propose strategies for increasing their participation in the national pool of kidney donors.

SHORTAGE OF AVAILABLE ORGANS

The major source of kidneys for African Americans have been derived from Caucasian cadaver donors. Among the kidney donors listed in 1993, 79 percent were from Caucasians as compared to 11 percent donated by African Americans. In reviewing the data further, to date, there has only been a 2 percent increase in African American donated kidneys since 1988 (United Network for Organ Sharing, 1994).

While the Caucasian population has been more willing to donate kidneys, there remains the persistent imbalance of supply and demand of available organs. As of May 1994, there were a total of 25,599 registrants on the national transplant waiting list for kidneys. Of this total, 34 percent or 8,693 registrants were identified as African Americans (United Network for Organ Sharing, 1994).

DONOR-RECIPIENT INCOMPATIBILITY

In addition to the shortage, there is also the problem of donor-recipient organ incompatibility. The distribution of ABO blood grouping and the major histocompatibility-complex (MHC) antigens are critical factors that influence organ donor-recipient matching. This in turn affects the probability of receiving a successful kidney transplant and lowers the incidence of organ rejection. In the literature there is extensive reporting on the differences along racial lines with respect to the criteria of ABO blood grouping and MHC compatibility (Akinlolu & Port, 1993; Kasiske et al., 1991; Lazda, 1992; Milford, Ratner, & Yunis, 1987; United States Renal Data System, 1993). The degree of compatibility for these criteria among Caucasians differs from African Americans. This further suggests a decreased probability for an excellent organ match and an increased possibility of organ rejection for the African American

ESRD patient. Together with the larger number of Caucasian donors, problems related to incompatibility, and the larger demand for kidneys, African Americans are at a clear disadvantage for being appropriately matched from the pool of available kidneys. This is particularly evident since the pool of African American donors (11%) is considerably smaller than their actual need for kidneys (34%) (United Network for Organ Sharing, 1994). Because African Americans have specific blood matching requirements that are unique to them, the probability of a better organ match could result from an African American recipient receiving a donor kidney from within the pool of African American donors.

WAITING PERIOD

Prior to undergoing a transplant procedure, potential kidney recipients are placed on a waiting list until they are properly matched with an available donor kidney. According to the United Network for Organ Sharing (1994), kidney registrants comprised 74 percent of all people on the national waiting list for various organs. The waiting list for kidney transplants has continued to increase over the years (United States Renal Data System, 1993). Although for all races, the percentage of registrants still waiting for a kidney has increased, there has been an alarming increase, from 7 percent in 1988 to 81 percent in 1993, of African Americans who continued to wait for a kidney. Furthermore, from 1988 to 1991 the waiting period for transplants increased from one to one- and one-half years. For African Americans the waiting time for being appropriately matched with a donor kidney is almost two times greater when compared to Caucasians (United Network for Organ Sharing, 1994).

For the specific population of ESRD patients, then, it is evident that quality of life and the threat of continued survival is influenced by the decreased availability of desired matched kidney donations and excess waiting time for the organ.

ATTITUDES OF AFRICAN AMERICANS TOWARD ORGAN DONATION

From a historical perspective, African Americans have been less willing to donate their organs. In the 1980s, Callender and his colleagues at Howard University were the first group to explore the reasons for the reluctance of African Americans to donate their kidneys (Callender et al., 1982). Their interest in this topic was sparked by the fact that non-blacks donated 41 of the 47 cadaver organs at the university's medical center. As a result, they conducted an exploratory-qualitative study, in which 40 black men and women were participants in group discussions on organ donation. Within this group, Callender et al. found six main reasons expressed for not donating kidneys: (1) lack of knowledge; (2) problems of communication between the medical and African American community; (3) mistrust of the medical community; (4) religious beliefs; (5) fear of surgery; and (6) prejudice. Although Callender et al. did not provide an indepth discussion of the findings, speculations for their implications are discussed in this chapter.

Lack of Knowledge

In general, the participant's in Callender's et al. (1982) study expressed having a need for more information about kidney transplants. The importance of increased communication and education were stressed as a vehicle for decreasing the general knowledge deficit about transplants. Although the specific types of knowledge deficits were not reported in this study, there are several domains of knowledge identified as necessary to communicate to African Americans, including: primary prevention; screening and early diagnosis; early treatment and compliance with the prescribed medical regimen; the incidence of ESRD among African Americans; transplantation as the treatment of choice for ESRD patients;

shortage of available organs; prolonged waiting period experienced by African American ESRD patients; matching and compatibility problems of African American recipients and potential Caucasian donors who are the main source of kidney organs; and the transplant protocol and convalescence.

Problem of Communication Between the Medical Community and Patients

Another theme that surfaced in the Callender et al. (1982) study was a concern regarding ability of physicians to adequately and appropriately discuss the importance of kidney donation to potential African American donors. They felt that the manner in which the subject of donation was approached greatly impacted on the willingness of people to donate organs. As in any physician-patient relationship, the importance of the physician's ability to discuss medical concerns and options in language and terms that are easily understood and culturally sensitive are extremely important. Likewise, patients should feel comfortable enough to ask questions and clarify information that they feel was unclear. This also includes their ability to approach sensitive subjects in a manner that is not disagreeable to the patient or family. In this light, the family should also be given the opportunity to ask questions and express concerns. This is particularly important when a grief stricken family is approached by a health professional to request an organ donation on behalf of their loved one.

Mistrust of the Medical Community

Mistrust of the medical community itself was another problem that was expressed by participants in Callender's et al. (1982) study. This concern was routed in the thought that individuals with donor cards would not receive adequate medical care if they entered a hospital that was actively seeking kidney donations. This concern is also related to the previous concern of communication problems among health care providers and the lay public. Furthermore, the relationship between hospitals and the communities in which they serve must be examined. In their attempts to provide quality care to the community, health care professionals and administrators must be sensitive to how they perceive and react to the health care attitudes expressed by the people they serve. Furthermore, they must be willing to reach out in a sustained way to keep the community well-informed and educated against misleading information or rumors. Without such an effort on the part of health care professionals and administrators, the imbalanced and dangerous situation that exists today will only increase in severity.

Fear of Surgery

Participants in Callender's et al. (1982) study also expressed, quite across the board, fear of having a surgical procedure. This concern has particular relevance to blood relative or non-relative living donors fearful about the ability to function with one kidney. Perhaps because human beings are born with two kidneys, they may feel that two kidneys are necessary for survival. They may also express concern with the possibility for developing postsurgical complications after donating a kidney. If something were to happen to their remaining kidney after donation, for instance, they may feel that their life would be threatened and they, too, would need a transplant in order to live. In view of these concerns, potential living donors need to be provided with factual information on the surgical procedure. They should be informed about potential complications no matter how small the risk. In this way they can make more informed decisions about donation based on current data.

Superstitious Beliefs

Although Callender et al. (1982) equated religion and superstitious beliefs as barriers against organ donation among African Americans, I will discuss this issue primarily within the context of their beliefs about life after death. Furthermore, in the Callender et al. study, there were no references to a particular religion which discourages organ donation or the nature of the superstition unique to this particular racial group. There were, however, reported concerns among African Americans about the importance of keeping the body whole for life after death. It can be further speculated that this thought was perhaps rooted in belief that the body would be mutilated during the process of organ removal. Study participants also expressed the belief that two kidneys were necessary for human survival and that removal would jeopardize life itself.

Racial Overtones

African Americans do seem to prefer to donate their kidneys to someone within their own race. Essentially, participants in the Callender et al. (1982) study felt that African American donated kidneys were far better than kidneys donated from persons of other races. Furthermore, it can be speculated that they felt that recipients from other races would be given preference to receive kidneys and subsequently benefit from receiving an organ of "exceptional" quality. In this example, it is clear that the context of racial overtones stems from the general state of misinformation about organ donation-recipient protocol. Furthermore, this preference for donation is not consistent with the criteria for appropriate organ matching. Again, the need for education here is critical to discourage incorrect information and to impact factual data about organ donation.

Because Callender et al. performed a qualitative study, there should be no attempts to apply those findings to the general population of African Americans. The data should be considered cautiously and used as a basis for further research. Not surprisingly, this seminal study was the springboard of future research that further examined the reluctance of African Americans to donate their kidneys. Some themes that were reported from the Callender et al. (1982) study are also similar and supported in later surveys of attitudinal barriers to organ donations among African Americans.

In a survey study of 111 African American participants, Roberts (1988) explored attitudes about their willingness to participate in organ donor programs. Similar to the Calender et al. (1982) study, the participants reported a lack of knowledge regarding the urgent need for black organ donors as well as the protocol for donation-transplantation surgical procedures.

In another study of 217 African American adults, Creecy and Wright (1990) reported significant correlations between the demographic variables of marital status and higher income African Americans to the willingness to donate organs. Willingness to donate was also significantly related to perceived need for transplants among blacks ($r = .14$, $p < .05$), confidence in physicians ($r = .22$, $p < .01$), perceived effectiveness of transplant organs ($r = .20$, $p < .01$), self-acceptance of transplant organs ($r = .23$, $p < .001$), and willingness to allow their own child to undergo transplant surgery ($r = .17$, $p < .01$). While these are not considered strong correlations, nevertheless they are still significant. As seen here, the issues of lack of knowledge about the need for transplants for African Americans, level of trust in the medical community, and knowledge level about the transplant procedure were factors common to earlier studies.

Davidson and Devney (1991), in their study of 187 African American adults, reported attitudinal barriers to organ donation to include religious beliefs and mistrust of the medical community. Strong religious beliefs against organ donations (beta $= -.32$, $p < .001$) and greater mistrust of the medical community (beta $= -.36$, $p < .001$) were inversely related to their willingness to donate their organs. In this study, the issue of strong religious beliefs is not specified or described. In absence of this clarification, it is difficult to determine whether the beliefs were associated with a particular religion and religiosity versus superstitious beliefs. On the other hand, as with previous studies, the issue of mistrust of the medical community is a persistent factor related to African American's reluctance toward organ donation.

A more recent study was conducted by The Gallup Organization (1993) for the Partnership for Organ Donation and the Harvard School of Public Health. In this study, 6,127 adults were studied to determine the public's attitude toward organ donation and transplantation. This was a telephone survey in which 10 percent of the participants were African American, 86 percent were Caucasian, and 4 percent were described as other. Overall, 78 percent of the respondents with greater than a high school education were very likely to donate their own organs as compared to 28 percent of those with a high school or less level of education. Table 1 depicts selected attitudes of only the Caucasians and African Americans from the study.

Overall, Caucasians were more aware and supportive of organ donation. They were also more likely to donate their organs or to have donor documentation. On the other hand, African Americans were more mistrustful of physicians, felt that organ donation was an experimental procedure, that it was important to be buried with the body intact, and that minority patients were racially discriminated against receiving organ transplants as needed. They also felt that the body would be marred as a result of the surgical procedure of organ donation.

The findings reported in this study were not surprisingly different from the previous studies mentioned. However, the researchers cautiously advise to interpret the data in a broad manner and to note that education was a variable that was positively associated toward organ donation across all racial lines.

Other demographic variables were also addressed in a study of public attitudes toward organ donation by Manninen and Evans

Table 1
Selected Attitudes of Caucasian's and African American's Attitudes Toward Organ Donation and Transplantation

	Caucasian	African Americans
1. Support the idea of donations of organs for transplant.	87%	69%
2. How likely are you to want to have your organs donated after your death?	39%	21%
3. Have you granted permission for organ donation on your driver's license or on a signed donor card?	30%	13%
4. Awareness of information about organ donation.	60%	43%
5. Strongly agree that doctors may *not* do everything possible before removing organs for transplantation.	5%	11%
6. Organ transplantation is an experimental medical procedure.	37%	54%
7. It is important for a person to have all his or her body parts when buried.	14%	38%
8. Strongly agree that they were worried that a loved one's body would be disfigured if their organs were donated.	17%	25%
9. Racial discrimination prevents minority patients from receiving the organ transplant they need.	26%	38%

Note: Adapted from the Gallup Organization, 1993, pp. 1–52.

(1985). The authors examined race and the likelihood toward organ donation. Thirty percent of the Caucasians were reported as more willing to donate their own and their relative's organs. In contrast, 13 percent of the participants referred to as "other races" were willing to donate. It can be speculated that African Americans were included in the "other race" category; however, it can not be assumed that they were exclusive to this category. In other words, it is unclear as to whether Hispanics or Asians were also included in this broad category of "other races." In view of this vague classification of race, the composition of this category remains unclear. The demographics of socioeconomics status and level of education were also examined. Participants with higher incomes ($40,000 +) and post high school education were more willing to have a current signed donor card and were more willing to donate their relative's organ.

Unfortunately, in most of the aforementioned studies, African Americans were studied as a homogenous group (Callender et al., 1982; Roberts, 1988; Davidson & Devney, 1991). The findings from these studies often lead to fixed conclusions that characterize the attitude of the entire African American community. The Gallup Organization (1993) and the studies conducted by Creecy and Wright (1990) and Manninen and Evans (1985) are examples of attempts to include sociodemographic variables to describe or explain the attitudes in this population. The findings of these studies suggest that the variables of marital status, education, and income may positively influence attitudes across racial lines. However, in the Manninen and Evans study, it is unclear why the authors classified the race of the sample as Caucasian and other races. It is also vague as to what racial groups comprised this category.

In reviewing the literature, the attitudes of African Americans toward organ donation has remained consistent over the years. From the early work of Callender et al. (1982) to a recent large scale survey conducted by The Gallup Organization (1993), there are several recurrent themes reported about reluctance to donate organs. Lack of information, mistrust of the medical community, fear of the surgical procedure and potential complications, and beliefs about death and burial are concerns generally expressed by the African American population.

STRATEGIES TO INCREASE DONOR PARTICIPATION

Ongoing efforts continue on the local, state, and national levels to address concerns discussed here and to develop interventions toward developing positive attitudes toward organ donations within the African American community. The strategies presented here are selected from among reported intervention projects across the United States (Callender, 1987a; Callender, 1987b; Callender, 1989; Callender et al., 1991; Hall et al., 1991; Kappel et al., 1993; Taylor & Hart, 1989).

The importance of education to increase awareness of the kidney donation-transplantation procedure and the need for African American kidney donors can not be over emphasized. In disseminating this information, the use of a variety of media strategies from an Afrocentric context should be maximized in the effort to bridge this knowledge gap.

Use of public address announcements in television, radio, newspapers, and magazines are useful informational sources. The content of the announcements must be tailored to specifically target the African American community and with an understanding that there are various subgroups within this population. A special effort should also focus on media that is heavily supported by members of the African American community. For example, in using television, attention to the subject of donation should be discussed or presented on African American oriented television shows, during their commercial air time, as well as African American oriented cable television stations such as Black Entertainment Television Network and religious stations.

Recommended as well are use of newspapers and magazines as additional media sources. As with television, public service messages may useful in local and African American-oriented newspapers and popular magazines.

Another available source for disseminating information includes various entry levels into the health care system set within particular African American communities or those that serve a large African American population. Clinics, physician offices, health screening programs, as well as hospital admission offices are all possible sites. Multileveled educational materials along with follow-up videotapes, group sessions, and one-on-one discussions on the need for donations can work toward the successful sharing of pertinent information. In response to giving potential donors and relatives of donors the opportunity to express their concerns, they should also receive empathetic understanding of their fears. It is important to keep in mind that the issues of quality of life, mortality, and life after death are charged with emotion, uncertainty, and sensitive feelings. Here, the ability of the health care professional to acknowledge, with care and sensitivity, all feelings by clients regarding the issues of concern is paramount. Approaching the possibility of donation in a positive manner, perhaps by referring to the donation as a "gift of life" that is unmeasurable on any level, can be helpful here. Special attention must also address patterns of communication, efforts toward establishing trustworthiness, as well as the avoidance of medical jargon which may contribute toward improving patient-provider relations. These suggestions may also be an effective way to allay fears about the procedure and decrease mistrust.

Using recognized leaders on the local, state, and national level as spokespersons is another rich source of disseminating information about organ donation-transplantation. Known artists from the entertainment arena, sports figures, politicians, and community leaders can all be effective communicators. A key influence in the African American community are the clergy. From a historical perspective, the church has always played a significant role in this community. In this instance, the clergy may be effective in inspiring feelings of altruism for the purpose of contributing to the quality of life of mankind as well as their own race. Other influential people may also include health care professionals such as African American nurses, physicians, social workers, or health care educators. Use of former African American kidney donors and/or recipients may be an emotional way of changing attitudes in the community.

Another approach may include the sponsoring of informational drives. These special efforts may be introduced on college campuses, and among African American sororities, fraternities, and civic and societal organizations. Information drives on college campuses were found by Manninen and Evans (1985) and The Gallup Organization (1993) as associated with increasing positive attitudes toward donation. Furthermore, organizations, such as the NAACP, and sororities, such as Alpha Kappa Alpha, have significant influences within African American communities and may be used as resources or sponsors for mobilizing drives for signing donor cards.

Professional health-related organizations whose membership traditionally comprised of African Americans may also contribute significantly toward educating the lay public, including: the National Medical Association, Black Nurse's Association, and the Association of Black Nursing Faculty in Higher Education. The members of these organizations can take a leadership role and be viewed as advocates for the lay public in the African American community.

Finally, there is the overall need to obtain sufficient financial support to forge an educational campaign on organ donation-transplantation. Sources of support may include the private sector, all levels of the government, business organizations, individual, and group volunteers.

REFERENCES

Akinlolu, O., & Port, F. (1993). Influence of race and gender on related donor renal transplantation rates. *American Journal of Kidney Diseases, 22,* 835–841.

Callender, C., Bayton, J., Yeager, C., & Clark, J. (1982). Attitudes among blacks for transplantation: A pilot project. *Journal of the National Medical Association, 74,* 807–809.

Callender, C. (1987a). Organ donation in blacks: A community approach. *Transplantation Proceedings, 19,* 1551–1554.

Callender, C. (1987b). Organ donation in black population: Where do we go from here. *Transplantation Proceedings, 19,* 36–40.

Callender, C. (1989). The results of transplantation in blacks: Just the tip of the iceberg. *Transplantation Proceedings, 21,* 3407–3410.

Callender, C., Hall, L., Yeager, C., Barber, J., Dunston, G., & Pinn-Wiggins, V. (1991). Special report: Organ donation and blacks. *The New England Journal of Medicine, 325,* 442–444.

Creecy, R., & Wright, R. (1990). Correlates of willingness to consider organ donation among blacks. *Social Science and Medicine, 31,* 1229–1232.

Davidson, M., & Devney, P. (1991). Attitudinal barriers to organ donation among black Americans. *Transplantation Proceedings, 23,* 2531–2532.

Evans, R., Bragg, C., & Bryan, F. (1981). A social and demographic profile of hemodialysis patients in the United States. *Journal of the American Medical Association, 245,* 487–491.

The Gallup Organization, Inc. (February, 1993). The American public's attitudes toward organ donation and transplantation. Conducted for *The Partnership for Organ Donation,* Boston, MA.

Hall, L., Callender, C., Yeager, C., Barber, J., Dunston, G., & Pinn-Wiggins, V. (1991). Organ donation in blacks: The next frontier. *Transplantation Proceedings, 23,* 2500–2504.

Kappel, D., Whitlock, M., Parks-Thomas, B., Hong, B., & Freedman, B. (1993). Increasing African American organ donation: The St. Louis experience. *Transplantation Proceedings, 25,* 2489–2490.

Kasiske, B., Neylan, F., Riggio, R., Danovitch, G., Kahana, L., Alexander, S., & White, M. (1991). The effect race on access and outcome in transplantation. *The New England Journal of Medicine, 324,* 302–307.

Lazda, V. (1992). The impact of HLA frequency differences races on the access to optimally HLA-matched cadaver renal transplants. *Transplantation, 53,* 352–357.

Livingston, I. (1993). Renal disease and black Americans: Selected issues. *Social Science Medicine, 37,* 613–621.

Manninen, D., & Evans, R. (1985). Public attitudes and behavior regarding organ donation. *The Journal of the American Medical Association, 253,* 3111–3115. Report.

Milford, E., Ratner, L., & Yunis, E. (1987). Will transplant immunogenetics lead to better graft survival in blacks? Racial variability in the accuracy of tissue typing for organ donation: The fourth american workshop. *Transplantation Proceedings, 19,* 30–32.

Prottas, J. (1983). Encouraging altruism: Public attitudes and marketing of organ donation. *Milbank Memorial Fund Quarterly, 61,* 278–305.

Roberts, K. (1988). Black American attitudes toward organ donation and transplantation. *Journal of the National Medical Association, 80,* 1121–1131.

Taylor, S., & Hart, C. (1989). Organ donation in blacks and minorities in Houston: Strategies for educating potential donor families. *Transplantation Proceedings, 21,* 3973–3974.

United Network for Organ Sharing. (May, 1994). *Technical Report.* Richmond, VA.

U.S. Bureau of the Census. (1993). *Statistical Abstract of the United States.* Washington, DC.: U.S. Government Printing Office.

U.S. Renal Data System. (1993). USRDS 1993 Annual Report. *The National Institutes of Health, National Institute of Diabetes and Digestive and Kidney Diseases,* Bethesda, MD.

Chapter Two

Cancer Among
African Americans

Sandra Millon-Underwood

I n spite of the many strides that have been made in the area of cancer prevention and control, the mere thought of cancer continues to evoke anxiety, fear, and uncertainty in the hearts and minds of most African Americans. The American Cancer Society (ACS) projected that in 1994 an estimated 1,209,000 Americans would be diagnosed with cancer. They projected that over 1,400 people a day, about 538,000 a year, would die from cancer (ACS, 1994). However, current national data indicate that among African Americans cancer incidence will be greater and cancer mortality will exceed that of the general population (ACS, 1991, 1994; Boring, Heath, & Squires, 1992; Clayton, & Byrd, 1993; PHS, 1990; USDHHS, 1986, 1989, 1991, 1992).

CANCER INCIDENCE, SURVIVAL, AND MORTALITY

Cancer, a group of diseases that is commonly characterized by uncontrolled growth, abnormal development of cells, and an unpredictable spread, is a major health problem in the African American community. African Americans have the highest overall incidence, lowest relative 5-year survival, and highest cancer mortality rate than any other ethnic population in the United States (ACS, 1991,

1994; Boring, Heath, & Squires, 1992; Byrd & Clayton, 1993; Clayton & Byrd, 1993; PHS, 1990; USDHHS, 1989, 1991, 1992).

Recent data show that African Americans have the highest incidence rates of cancer of female breast (for women under age 40), cervix uteri, corpus uteri, oral cavity, esophagus, colon, larynx, lung (male), multiple myeloma, pancreas, and prostate (ACS, 1994; Boring, Heath, & Squires, 1992; Byrd & Clayton, 1993; Clayton & Byrd, 1993; PHS, 1990; USDHHS, 1986, 1989) (see Table 1, pp. 52–53). The relative 5-year survival rate for African Americans diagnosed with cancer from 1983 through 1990 was approximately 35 percent compared with 55 percent for whites (ACS, 1991, 1994). In addition, the data indicate that African Americans have the lowest 5-year survival rate for cancers of the cervix uteri, corpus uteri, and esophagus (ACS, 1994; Boring, Heath, & Squires, 1992; Byrd & Clayton, 1993; Clayton & Byrd, 1993; PHS, 1990; USDHHS, 1986, 1989, 1990) (see Table 2, p. 54).

Cancer is the second leading cause of death among African Americans (see Table 3, p. 55). Over the past 30 years, the age adjusted cancer mortality rate for African American men is reported to have increased from 21 percent to 66 percent above the rate for all races; while the rate for African American women is reported to have increased from being marginally below the rate for all races to 10 percent above it (ACS, 1991; Boring, Heath, & Squires, 1992; Boyd, 1989; Byrd & Clayton, 1993; Clayton & Byrd, 1993; Hardy, 1991; PHS, 1990; USDHHS, 1986, 1989) (see Tables 4–12, pp. 56–64).

The discrepancies in cancer incidence among African Americans and the general population are said to often be the result of a multitude of external (chemical, radiation, and viruses), internal (hormones, immune conditions, and inheritable mutations), and socioeconomic factors. Lifestyle preferences, habits, and behaviors that contribute to cancer risk have similarly been reported to significantly influence these trends (ACS, 1991, 1994; Boring, Heath, & Squires, 1992; Byrd & Clayton, 1993; Clayton & Byrd, 1993; PHS, 1990; USDHHS, 1986, 1989).

Many of the cancers afflicting African Americans represent cancers for which screening tests are available or which present symptoms early in the disease process. Nevertheless, a considerable part of the variation in survival has been reported to be directly related to late diagnosis. It has been suggested that perceptions, beliefs, and fear regarding cancer, cancer diagnosis, cancer care, in addition to the lack of sufficient resources for health care, have significantly influenced health behavior and have indirectly effected the stage at which cancer is diagnosed among African Americans. Significant here as well is the fact that, once diagnosed and under medical care, the range and intensity of cancer treatment prescribed for African Americans are often described as less aggressive than, for example, for whites (ACS, 1991; Brawn, 1993; Hunter, 1993, PHS, 1990; Polednak, 1992; USDHHS, 1986, 1989, 1991).

The variations in cancer mortality among African Americans are noted to be due to higher cancer incidence, later stage of disease at time of first treatment, less aggressive cancer treatment, and limitations in the availability of resources to cope with illness (ACS, 1990, Boring, Heath, & Squires, 1992; Byrd & Clayton, 1993; Clayton & Byrd, 1993; Dixon & Wilson, 1994; Hardy, 1991; USDHHS, 1991). The overrepresentation of those of low socioeconomic status within the population have also been reported to hinder cancer care resulting in higher cancer mortality rates.

KNOWLEDGE, ATTITUDES, AND CANCER CARE AMONG AFRICAN AMERICANS

Knowledge, beliefs, attitudes, and perceptions are known to play an integral role in cancer prevention and control among African Americans. Certainly, in order to take appropriate action a person must have correct information regarding prevention, early detection and treatment, the correct perception regarding the efficacy of cancer prevention and control interventions, trust in their health care provider, and confidence in the current state of the health care system at large. Insufficiencies in any or all of these factors have been observed to significantly effect the health behaviors of African Americans and impede their involvement in various cancer prevention and control activities.

Frequently reported in the literature as well are so-called prevailing attitudes of pessimism and fatalism regarding cancer among African American men and women. The literature suggests that, while African Americans often acknowledge the severity of the disease, they tend to underestimate its incidence, are pessimistic about cure, and are generally hesitant to seek medical advice when symptoms suggestive of cancer occur (ACS, 1980, CIS, 1983, Loehrer, 1991; NCI, 1983, 1986; Thomas, 1993; USDHHS, 1986, 1989).

In the early 1930s, the American Cancer Society initiated a national campaign to familiarize the public with common warning signs for cancer (see Figure 1). Despite their attempts to educate the public of the signs and symptoms most commonly associated with cancer, most African Americans were reported as remaining uninformed (ACS, 1980, CIS, 1983, Loehrer, 1991; NCI, 1983, 1986; Robinson, 1991; Thomas, 1993; USDHHS, 1986, 1989, 1991, 1992). Similar programs were initiated by the Society and other national agencies and organizations to educate the public on programs recommended for cancer screening (see Figure 2). However, in this instance as well, African Americans were noted to be less likely to be aware of early detection and screening protocols (ACS, 1980, 1981; Cardwell & Collier, 1981; Denniston, 1981; Hall & Bell, 1985; Jones, 1989; Loehrer, 1991; Michielutte & Dieseker, 1982; Price, Desmond, & Wallace, 1988; Robinson, 1991; USDHHS, 1986, 1989).

Many African Americans dismiss the potential of developing cancer as an immediate cause for concern (ACS, 1992; Bloom, Hayes, Saunder, & Flatt, 1987; Denniston, 1981; Hall & Bell, 1985; Underwood, 1992; Underwood & Sanders, 1991). Daily

Figure 1
Cancer Warning Signs 1930 and 1994

HERE ARE THE
DANGER SIGNALS
THAT MAY MEAN
CANCER

1. Any lump in the breast or other part of the body, especially one which begins to grow or change.
2. Any sore which does not heal, particularly on the face or in the mouth.
3. Any unusual discharge or bleeding from any part of the body.

PAIN IS A LATE SYMPTOM

If you have suspicious symptoms secure competent medical advice without delay.

Many Cancers Can Be Cured
by Early Treatment

The Seven Danger Signals of Cancer

- ○ Unusual bleeding or discharge.
- ○ A lump or thickening in the breast or elsewhere.
- ○ A sore throat that does not heal.
- ○ Change in bowel or bladder habits.
- ○ Hoarseness or cough.
- ○ Indigestion or difficulty in swallowing.
- ○ Change in a wart or mole.

THE AMERICAN CANCER SOCIETY

The American Cancer Society is the only national voluntary agency fighting cancer through research, education, and service to the cancer patient.

The American Cancer Society is yours and needs you in the fight against cancer.

Figure 2
Recommended Cancer Screening Tests
for Asymptomatic People (1992)

SUMMARY OF
AMERICAN CANCER SOCIETY RECOMMENDATIONS FOR
THE EARLY DETECTION OF CANCER
IN ASYMPTOMATIC PEOPLE

Test or Procedure	Population		
	Sex	Age	Frequency
Sigmoidoscopy	M & F	50 and over	Every 3 to 5 years based on advice of physician
Stool Guaiac Slide Test	M & F	Over 50	Every year
Digital Rectal Examination	M & F	Over 40	Every year
Pap Test	F	All women who are or who have been sexually active, or have reached age 18, should have an annual Pap test and pelvic examination. After a woman has had three or more consecutive satisfactory normal annual examinations, the Pap test may be performed less frequently at the discretion of her physician.	
Pelvic Examination	F	18–40	Every 1–3 years with Pap test
		Over 40	Every year
Endometrial Tissue Sample	F	At menopause Women at high risk*	At menopause
Breast Self-examination	F	20 and older	Every month
Breast Clinical Examination	F	20–40	Every 3 years
		Over 40	Every year
Mammography**	F	40–49	Every 1–2 years
		50 & over	Every year
Health Counseling and	M & F	Over 20	Every 3 years
Cancer Checkup***	M & F	Over 40	Every year

*History of infertility, obesity, failure to ovulate, abnormal uterine bleeding, or estrogen therapy.
**Screening mammography should begin by age 40.
***To include examination for cancers of the thyroid, testicles, prostate, ovaries, lymph nodes, oral region, and skin.   1/92

anxieties about economic conditions, discrimination, and health problems often are described as taking precedence over concerns regarding cancer, unless that person has experienced the disease personally. Having often been bombarded with not only too much information about cancer, but also information that is often contradictory and sensationalized, African Americans are often described as putting little credence in much of the information that is disseminated.

Numerous reports suggest that many African Americans have never heard of mammography, digital rectal examination, blood stool analysis, or proctoscopic examination by these or other terms (ACS, 1980, 1981; Cardwell & Collier, 1981; Denniston, 1981; Durack, 1989; Gullatte, 1993; Hall & Bell, 1985; Jones, 1989; Loehrer, 1991; Price, Desmond, & Wallace, 1988; Underwood & Sanders, 1990; USDHHS, 1989; Winn & Dimery, 1988). In addition, there appears to be a general lack of understanding that the procedures are recommended in the absence of problems or symptoms.

Although breast self-examination, mammography, and pap smears are becoming more frequently utilized than was true in the early 1980s, significant under-utilization by African Americans is still noted (Bang, Perlin, & Sampson, 1987; Chow, Liff, & Greenberg, 1988; Huguley, 1987; Lauver, 1992; Price, 1992; USDHHS, 1986, 1989, 1991, 1992). Significant degrees of under-utilization have also been observed in the area of uterine, colon, and prostate cancer screening.

Data show that fewer African Americans believe tobacco, diet, sunshine, and x-rays influence cancer risk (Brownson, 1992; NCI, 1983, 1987). Many do not realize that bumps, bruises, touching ones sexual organs, and fluorinated or chlorinated water do not increase chances of getting cancer (Cardwell & Collier, 1981; CIS, 1983; Jones, 1989; Loehrer, 1991; NCI, 1983, 1986; Price, Desmond, & Wallace, 1988; USDHHS, 1986, 1989). In addition, among many African Americans, there is still a prevailing acceptance of the myth that cancer is contagious, that air causes cancer to spread, that surgery will cause cancer to metastasize, and that home remedies and alternative modalities are just as good, or better, than state-of-the-art treatments for controlling cancer and its sequel (ACS, 1980; CIS, 1983; Dixon & Wilson, 1994; Loehrer, 1991; NCI, 1983, 1986; Snow, 1993; USDHHS, 1986, 1989; Williams, 1975).

Throughout their history, African Americans have experienced difficulty interacting with and accessing resources within the health care delivery system. Often residing in locations far removed from services of medical care, unable to pay for care in medical systems stressing fee for service, having been become frustrated by recurring incidents of discrimination and abuse, lacking sufficient insurance to cover health care costs, and receiving less adequate care, African Americans are described as having become more tolerant of illness and disease, less reliant on western medicine, and less likely to utilize ambulatory, in-patient, and extended care facilities for cancer care or other health-related conditions (Abraham, 1993; Bailey, 1989; Dixon & Wilson, 1994; Washington, 1994).

EFFECT OF LIFESTYLE PREFERENCES, HABITS, AND BEHAVIORS ON THE CANCER RISK OF AFRICAN AMERICANS

The U.S. Surgeon General identified cigarette smoking as the chief, single, avoidable cause of death in the United States (USDHHS, 1989). Nevertheless, there are 49 million smokers in the United States of which approximately 6 million are African American. Compared with other ethnic groups, African Americans tend to be lighter smokers in terms of years of smoking. The smoking practices of African American women are noted to be similar to those of white women (23.4% and 21.2%, respectively). However, smoking practices of the African American males are reported to have the highest smoking prevalence of any group (see Table 13, pp. 65–66) (Ansell, 1993; Day, 1993; Dixon & Wilson, 1994; Geronimus, 1993; Kabat, 1991; Manfredi, 1992; NCHS, 1990; USDHHS, 1989; Van, 1992). In addition, while it is not clear if the consequences are behavioral or biological, tobacco-related cancers are said to account for approximately 45 percent of the new cancer cases in African American men, and 25 percent in African American females. It has also been suggested that 37 percent of the cancer deaths in African American males and 20 percent of the cancer deaths in African American females are directly linked to tobacco (ACS, 1994; Boring, Heath, & Squires, 1992; USDHHS, 1989, 1991, 1992).

An estimated 35 percent of all cancers in the United States are said to be attributable to diet. While the USDHHS reports that many food factors must be considered when identifying dietary risk, the disproportionate consumption of foods high in fats, at the expense of vitamin-rich foods high in complex carbohydrates and fiber, are among the primary culprits (Cotunga, 1992, Dixon & Wilson, 1994; USDHHS, 1989).

There is no single generalization that can adequately describe the dietary trends among African Americans. Diet variations among those within the African American community are extensive. Their dietary trends are determined largely by regional, cultural, religious, and historical factors, as those of other racial/cultural groups. However, there is a tendency among African Americans toward dietary patterns which result in vitamin-poor, nitrate-rich, low fiber and high saturated fat intake (Dixon & Wilson, 1994; USDHHS, 1986) (Tables 14, 15, 16, pp. 67–69).

Alcohol consumption has also been linked to the development of cancer. Persons, especially those who are also cigarette smokers or tobacco chewers, are reported to be at an unusually high risk for developing cancer of the mouth, throat, larynx, esophagus, and liver (ACS, 1991, 1994).

Drinking patterns differ according to gender, race, ethnicity, and cultural background. However, national data indicate that for African Americans the risk for developing alcohol-related cancer is significant given that over 50 percent of the male population and over 30 percent of the female population between the ages of 18 and 64 are described as "drinkers" (Darrow, 1992; Day, 1993; Dixon & Wilson, 1994; USDHHS, 1991) (see Table 17, pp. 70–71).

Because significant percentages of African Americans reside in cities, with high concentrations living within the inner city, they are exposed to a relatively greater number of environmental hazards than non-minorities (USDHHS, 1986, 1991, 1992). Occupational studies also document that African Americans, and persons from other racial and ethnic groups, are employed disproportionately in high-risk occupations (USDHHS, 1986, 1991, 1992). While African Americans in the workforce are highly concentrated in blue collar and service related occupations, discriminatory work assignments and the inclusion of African Americans in less skilled jobs have increased the frequency in which they are assigned to more hazardous worksites, thereby increasing their exposure to substances which are known to significantly compromise health (USDHHS, 1985).

Exposure to carcinogenic agents such as lead, nickel, chromate, asbestos, vinyl chloride, pesticides, or herbicides are known to increase a person's risk for developing various cancer. Nevertheless, African Americans, more often than persons from other non-minority groups, have had higher exposures to these substances via environmental and occupational channels (USDHHS, 1986, 1991, 1992).

THE EFFECT OF SOCIOECONOMIC STATUS ON CANCER PREVENTION AND CONTROL

For virtually all chronic diseases, including cancer, economic disadvantage is a special risk factor. According to the most recent national statistics, the incidence of cancer increases as family income decreases (ACS, 1990; PHS, 1990; Rogers, 1992; Sorlier, 1992;

USDHHS, 1991, 1992). While the incidence varies across sites, the cancers which occur most frequently among the poor are lung, esophageal, oral, cervical, and prostate (ACS, 1990; PHS, 1990). Five-year cancer survival rates are also lower for the economically and medically disadvantaged (ACS, 1990; PHS, 1990). In addition, the cancer mortality of the poor is significantly higher compared with people with incomes above the poverty line (ACS, 1990; PHS, 1990; USDHHS, 1991).

According to the Public Health Service (1990), one in every eight Americans lives in a family whose income falls below the federal poverty level. However, for African Americans one in three live in a family whose income falls below the poverty level (see Table 18, pp. 72–73) (ACS, 1990; PHS, 1990). In addition, the combined effect of economic disadvantage, medical disadvantage, and indigenous cultural factors often significantly increase cancer risk and impede access to the many cancer prevention, early detection, treatment, and rehabilitation services provided through the health care system (thereby further contributing to disparities in health status as discussed here).

REDUCING CANCER AMONG AFRICAN AMERICANS: THE CHALLENGE

The greatest potential for reducing cancer mortality among African Americans, and other at-risk groups, may be realized through aggressive implementation of comprehensive education, prevention, diagnostic, and treatment programs. While all eligible persons should have the opportunity to benefit from enrollment in such programs, at present there is a disproportionate under-representation of African Americans, and other special populations, in investigational programs and/or clinical trials (ACS, 1991; Hunter, Frelick, & Feldman, 1987; Svensson, 1989). Among the many factors assumed to contribute to this situation are (1) the hesitancy of many African

Americans to participate in research, (2) the lack of information disseminated by many of health care providers of cancer programs and trials, (3) the lack of knowledge of most in the African American community of the opportunities for (and benefits of) participation in cancer programs and trials, (4) the unwillingness of many in the African American community to consider cancer programs and trials as a preventive, diagnostic or treatment option, and (5) the historical barriers that have left life-threatening impressions that linger in the minds of minorities, especially African Americans.

Mindful of the "deadly experiments" that were conducted on African Americans in the 1930s, many African Americans believe that if they agree to participate in an investigational program they will not be appropriately, completely, and honestly informed of the nature of the risks or the benefits (Allen, 1915; Brunner, 1915; Fort, 1915; Hindman, 1915; Ingelfinger, 1972; Kampmeir, 1972; Lee, 1915; Rivers, 1953). There is a fear that they would be deliberately assigned to a non-intervention group when promising options are available. There is also the belief that they would be subjected to interventions without their knowledge.

Many African Americans fear that if they participate in an investigational program or trial, placebos would be substituted for lifesaving interventions, that interventions with proven efficacy would be deliberately withheld, or that they would not receive a full course of treatment (Allen, 1915; Byman, 1991; Caplan, Edgar, King, & Jones, 1992; Cary, 1992; Guillory, 1987; Jones, 1981; Junod, 1993; Underwood, Davis, & Sanders, 1993; Washington, 1994). In addition, there is the fear that vital interventions would be abruptly discontinued if funding sources for implementing the investigational protocol are no longer available.

In 1990, the U.S. Department of Health and Human Services established a set of national health goals to be achieved by the year 2000, *Healthy People 2000*. In addition to these goals, age, gender, race and ethnically specific objectives and strategies geared towards health promotion, health protection, and increasing the utilization of health related services were identified (see Figure 3).

Figure 3
National Health Goals for the Year 2000

- Increase the span of healthy life for all Americans
- Decrease health disparities among Americans
- Achieve access to preventive services for all Americans

Among African Americans, specific objectives and strategies have been identified to facilitate cancer prevention and control. It has been suggested that modification in certain lifestyles, habits, behaviors, and health care practices would significantly reduce cancer incidence, decrease mortality, and increase survivorship (ACS, 1992; NCI, 1989; NIH, 1987; USDHHS, 1986, 1989; see Figure 4). Changes advocated include:

1. Cessation of smoking and tobacco use;
2. Modifying the diet to increase fiber and reduce fat;
3. Participating in cancer screening and follow-up; and
4. Increasing enrollment in preventative, diagnostic/screening and treatment programs and trials.

Health care professionals working with African Americans on an ongoing basis can, and should, assume a major responsibility for planning, implementing, and evaluating cancer prevention and control programs designed to meet the needs of the African American community. Their increased familiarity with African American lifestyles, values, and beliefs make them more uniquely qualified to serve in this capacity. This group (compared to those without such ongoing contact) more often possess a greater knowledge and sensitivity regarding the cultural, ethnic, and socioeconomic factors that influence lifestyles, habits, behaviors, health knowledge, beliefs, attitudes, and health care practices of African Americans. Such awareness and sensitivity is frequently documented as essential for

Figure 4
Percent of Cancers Diagnosed in Localized Stage by Race

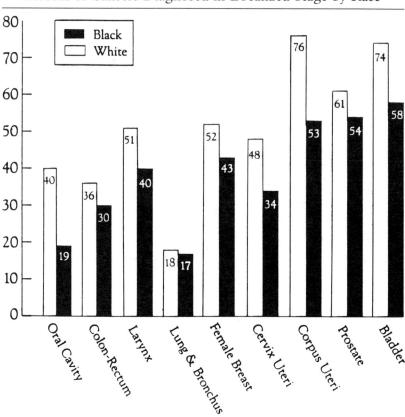

*Local—cancer is diagnosed when still confined to the organ or origin.
Source: Cancer Statistics Branch, NCI.

transcending the various barriers effecting preventive health-seeking behaviors (Hayes, 1991; Jones, 1989; Lacey, 1989; Phillips, 1991; Underwood & Sanders, 1990; Willis, 1989). As a result, they are deemed to be invaluable in the identification and counseling of those at risk, and in disseminating updated information as it relates to cancer prevention and control.

Most Americans believe that cancer incidence and mortality can be reduced by alleviating the problems that currently exist in accessibility to health care. However, it must be remembered that many factors have been noted to contribute to these cancer trends among African Americans. Therefore, if progress is to be made, it will depend on how well all pertinent factors are addressed, both individually and collectively.

All the treatment advances in the world do nothing for a patient who does not know about them, cannot get to where they are available, or does nothing because of fear.

L. Jones, 1988

REFERENCES

Abraham, L. (1993). *Mama might be better off dead. The failure of health care in urban America.* Chicago, IL: University of Chicago Press.

Allen, L. C. (1915). The Negro health problem. *American Journal of Public Health, 5*(3), 194–205.

American Cancer Society. (1994). Cancer facts and figures. Atlanta, GA: American Cancer Society.

American Cancer Society. (1992). Cancer in African Americans. *Ca-A Journal for Clinicians, 42*(1), 5–18.

American Cancer Society. (1991). *Cancer facts and figures for minority Americans.* Atlanta, GA: American Cancer Society.

American Cancer Society. (1991). *Clinical trials for the treatment of cancer.* Atlanta, GA: American Cancer Society.

American Cancer Society. (1990). *Cancer and the socioeconomically disadvantaged.* Atlanta, GA: American Cancer Society.

American Cancer Society. (1981). *Black Americans' attitudes towards cancer and cancer tests: Highlights of a study. Ca-A Journal for Clinicians, 31,* 212–218.

American Cancer Society, EVAXX, Inc. (1980). *A study of black attitudes towards cancer and cancer tests.* New York: American Cancer Society.

Ahijeych, K., & Bernhard, L. (1994). Health-promoting behaviors of African American women. *Nursing Research, 43*(2), 86–89.

Ansell, D. (1993). Race and sex differences in lung cancer risk associated with cigarette smoking. *International Journal of Epidemiology, 22*(4), 592–599.

Bailey, E. (1989). Sociocultural factors and health care seeking behavior among black Americans. *Journal of the National Medical Association, 79*(4), 389–392.

Bang, K. M., Perlin, E., & Sampson, C. C. (1987) Increase cancer risks in blacks: A look at the factors. *Journal of the National Medical Association, 70*(4), 383–388.

Bloom, J., Hayes, W., Saunder, F., & Flatt, S. (1987). Cancer awareness and secondary prevention practices in black Americans: Implications for intervention. *Family and Community Health, 109*(3), 19–20.

Boring, C., Heath, C., & Squires, T. (1992). Cancer statistics for African Americans, 1992. *Ca-A Journal for Clinicians, 42*(1), 19–38.

Boyd, J. (1989). Black's at 11% greater cancer risk. *Cancer Letter, 15*(1), 1–2.

Brawn, P. (1993). Stage at presentation and survival of white and black patients with prostatic carcinoma. *Cancer, 71*(8), 2569–2573.

Brownson, R. (1992). Demographic and socioeconomic differences in the beliefs about the health effects of smoking. *American Journal of Public Health, 82*(1), 99–103.

Brunner, W. (1915). The Negro health problem in southern cities. *American Journal of Public Health, 5*(3), 183–191.

Byman, B. (1991). Out from the shadow of Tuskegee. *Minnesota Medicine, 74*(8), 15–20.

Byrd, W., & Clayton, L. (1993). The African American cancer crisis: A prescription. *Journal of Health Care for the Poor and Underserved, 4*(2), 102–116.

Caplan, A., Edgar, H., King, P., & Jones, J. (1992). Twenty years after: The legacy of the Tuskegee Syphilis Study. *Hastings Center Report, 22*(6), 29–40.

Cary, L. (1992). Why it's not just paranoia: An American history of "plans" for blacks. *Newsweek, 69*(14), 23.

Cancer Information Service. (1983). Preliminary report from the black audience outreach task force. Presented to the Cancer Communications Network Meeting.

Cardwell, J., & Collier, W. (1981). Racial differences in cancer awareness. *Urban Health, 81,* 29–31.

Chow, W. H. Liff, J. M., & Greenberg, R. S. (1988). Mammography in Atlanta. *Journal of the Medical Association of Georgia, 76,* 788–792.

Clayton, L., & Byrd, W. (1993). The African American cancer crisis: The problem. *Journal of Health Care for the Poor and Underserved, 4*(2), 83–101.

Cotunga, N. (1992). Nutrition and cancer prevention knowledge, beliefs and practices: 1987 National Health Interview Survey. *Journal of the American Dietetic Association, 92*(8), 963–968.

Darrow, S. (1992). Sociodemographic characteristics of alcohol consumption among African American and white women. *Women's Health, 18*(4), 35–51.

Day, G. (1993). Racial differences in risk of oral and pharangeal cancer. *Journal of the National Cancer Institute, 85*(6), 465–473.

Denniston, R. (1981). Cancer knowledge, attitudes and practices between black Americans. *Progress in Clinical Biological Research, 83,* 225–235.

Dixon, B., & Wilson, J. (1994). *Good health for African Americans.* New York: Crown.

Durack, R. C. et al. (1989) Detroit's avoidable mortality project: Breast cancer control for inner-city women. *Public Health Report, 104*(6), 327–535.

Fort, A. J. (1915). The Negro health problem in rural communities. *American Journal of Public Health, 5*(3), 191–193.

Geronimus, A. (1993). Age pattern of smoking in United States black and white women of childbearing age. *American Journal of Public Health, 83*(9), 1258–1264.

Guillory, J. (1987). Ethnic perspective on cancer nursing: The black American. *Oncology Nursing Forum, 14*(1), 66–69.

Gullatte, M. (1993). Cancer prevention and early detection. In J. Otto (Ed.), *Cancer nursing* (2nd Ed.). New York: Mosby.

Hall, H., & Bell, X. (1985). Increases in cancer rates between blacks. *Journal of Black Psychology, 12,* 1–14.

Hardy, R. (1991). Cancer prognosis in black Americans. *Journal of the National Medical Association, 83*(7), 574–579.

Hayes, M. (1991). Making cancer prevention effective for African Americans. *Statistical Bulletin of Metropolitan Life Insurance Company, 72,* 18–22.

Hindman, S. S. (1915). Syphilis among insane Negros. *American Journal of Public Health, 5*(3), 218–224.

Huguley, C. M. (1987). Screening for breast cancer. *Journal of the Medical Association of Georgia, 16*(5), 310–313.

Hunter, C. (1993). Breast cancer: Factors associated with stage at diagnosis in black and white women. *Journal of the National Cancer Institute, 85*(14), 1129–1137.

Hunter C. P., Frelick, R. W., Feldman, A. R. et al. (1987). Selection factors in clinical trials: Results from the Community Clinical Oncology Program physician's log. *Cancer Treatment Report, 71,* 499–565.

Indelfinger, F. (1972). Informed (but uneducated) consent. *New England Journal of Medicine, 287*(9), 465–466.

Junod, T. (1993). Deadly medicine. *Gentleman's Quarterly, 63*(6), 164–171, 231–234.

Jones, J. H. (1981). *Bad blood.* New York: Free Press.

Jones, L. A. (1989). *Minorities and cancer.* New York: Springer-Verlag.

Jones, L. A. (1988). Realities of cancer in minority communities. *Cancer Bulletin, 40*(2), 70.

Kabat, G. (1991). Use of mentholated cigarettes and lung cancer risk. *Cancer Research, 51*(24), 6510–6513.

Kampmeir, R. H. (1972). The Tuskegee study of un-treated syphilis. *Southern Medical Journal, 65*(10), 1247–1451.

Lacey, L. P. et al. (1989). An urban community-based cancer prevention screening and health education intervention in Chicago. *Public Health Reports, 104*(6), 536–541.

Lauver, D. (1992). Psychosocial variables, race and intention to seek care for breast cancer symptoms. *Nursing Research, 41*(4), 236–241.

Lee, L. (1915). The Negro as a problem in public health charity. *American Journal of Public Health, 5*(3), 205–211.

Loehrer, P. (1991). Knowledge and beliefs about cancer in a socioeconomically disadvantaged population. *Cancer, 68,* 1665–1671.

Manfredi, C. (1992). Smoking-related behavior, beliefs and social environment of young black women in subsidized public housing in Chicago. *American Journal of Public Health, 82*(2), 267–272.

Michielutte, R., & Diseker, R. (1982). Racial differences in knowledge of cancer: A pilot study. *Social Science Medicine, 16,* 245–253.

National Cancer Institute. (1989). Proceeding of the National Cancer Institute National black Leadership Initiative on Cancer, Meeting of the Regional Leadership. Bethesda, MD.

National Cancer Institute. (1983). *Technical report: Cancer prevention awareness survey.* Bethesda, MD: National Cancer Institute Office of Cancer Communication.

National Cancer Institute. (1986). *Technical report: Cancer prevention awareness survey.* Bethesda, MD: National Cancer Institute Office of Cancer Communication.

National Cancer Institute. (1986). *Cancer among blacks and other minorities: Statistical profiles.* Washington, DC: National Cancer Institutes.

National Center for Health Statistics. (1990). Health promotion and disease prevention, United States 1990, *Vital and Health Statistics, 10*(185).

National Institutes of Health. (1987). *Diet, nutrition and cancer prevention: A guide to food choices.* Bethesda, MD: USDHHS, Public Health Service.

Phillips, J. (1991). Cancer control by the year 2000: Implications for action. *Journal of the National Black Nurses' Association, 5,* 42–48.

Polednak, A. (1992). Black vs. white racial differences in client stage at diagnosis and treatment of prostate cancer. *Cancer, 70*(8), 2152–2158.

Price, J. (1992). Urban black women's perceptions of breast cancer and mammograms. *Journal of Community Health, 17*(4), 191–204.

Price, J., Desmond, S., & Wallace, M. (1988). Black Americans' perceptions of cancer. *Journal of the National Medical Association, 80*(12), 1297–1304.

Public Health Service. (1990). Summary of healthy people 2000: National health promotion and disease prevention objectives. Washington, DC: American Public Health Association.

Rivers, E. (1953). Twenty years of follow-up experience in a long-range medical study. *Public Health Reports, 68*(4), 391–395.

Robinson, R. (1991). Cancer awareness among African Americans. *Journal of the National Medical Association, 83*(6), 491–497.

Rogers, R. (1992). Living and dying in the United States: Sociodemographic determinants of deaths among Blacks and Whites. *Demography, 29*(2), 287–303.

Sorlie, P. (1992). Black-white mortality differences by family income. *Lancet, 340*(815), 346–350.

Snow, L. (1993). *Walkin' over medicine: Traditional health practices in African-American life.* Boulder, CO: Westview.

Svensson, C. (1989). Representation of American blacks in clinical trials of new drugs. *Journal of the National Medical Association, 261*(2), 263–265.

Thomas, S. (1993). Cancer awareness and attitudes towards preventive health behavior. *Journal of the Louisiana State Medical Society, 145*(4), 139–145.

Underwood, S. (1992). Cancer risk reduction and early detection behaviors among African-American men: Focus on learned helplessness. *Journal of Community Health Nursing, 9*(1), 21–31.

Underwood, S., David, M., & Sanders, E. (1993). Determinants of participation in state-of-the-art cancer prevention, early detection, screening and treatment trials among African Americans. *Cancer Nursing, 16*(1), 25–33.

Underwood, S., & Sanders, E. (1991). Perceptual determinants of cancer risk reduction and early detection behavior among African-American men. *Cancer Nursing, 14*(6), 281–288.

Underwood, S., & Sanders, E. (1990). Factors contributing to health promotion behaviors among African-American men. *Oncology Nursing Forum, 17*(5), 707–712.

USDHHS. (1992). Healthy United States and healthy people 200 review. Bethesda, MD: USDHHS.

USDHHS. (1991). Health status of minorities and low income groups. Bethesda, MD: USDHHS.

USDHHS. (1989). *Cancer statistics review* (1973–1986). Bethesda, MD: USDHHS.

USDHHS. (1986). *Report of the Secretary's Task Force on black & minority health.* Bethesda, MD: USDHHS.

USDHHS. (1986). *Cancer among blacks and other minorities.* Bethesda, MD: USDHHS.

USDHHS. (1986). Cross-cultural counseling: A guide for nutrition and health counselors. Bethesda, MD: USDHHS.

Van, J. (1992, November 19). Study finds blacks are less addicted to smoking. *Chicago Tribune, 1,* 5.

Washington, H. (1994). Of mice and men. *Emerge, 6*(1), 24–38.

Weinrish, S. (1992). Knowledge of colorectal cancer among older adults. *Cancer Nursing, 15*(5), 322–330.

Williams, R. (1975). *Textbook of black-related diseases.* New York: McGraw-Hill.

Willis, M. (1989). Interagency collaboration: Teaching breast self-examination to black women. *Oncology Nursing Forum, 16*(2), 171–177.

Winn, R. E., & Dimery, I. W. (1988). Cancer prevention and detection projects among minorities: National Cancer Institute initiatives. *Cancer Bulletin, 40*(2), 75–78.

Table 1

Cancer Incidence Rates by Race and Gender

Data are based on the Surveillance, Epidemiology, and End Results Program's population-based registries in Atlanta, Detroit, Seattle-Puget Sound, San Francisco-Oakland, Connecticut, Iowa, New Mexico, Utah, and Hawaii.

Race, Sex, and Site	1973	1975	1980	1985	1986	1987	1988	1989	1990	Estimated Annual Percent Change[1]
				Number of New Cases per 100,000 Population[2]						
White Male										
All sites	363.0	378.5	405.7	428.1	434.3	452.5	448.0	451.8	464.9	1.3
Oral cavity and pharynx	17.5	18.3	16.9	16.7	16.2	17.2	15.4	15.1	15.8	-0.8
Esophagus	4.8	4.8	4.9	5.3	5.2	5.4	5.4	5.1	6.0	0.9
Stomach	13.9	12.5	12.3	10.5	10.8	10.5	10.7	10.7	9.2	-1.7
Colon and rectum	54.1	55.0	58.5	63.4	62.0	61.1	59.3	58.6	58.0	0.5
Colon	34.7	36.1	39.2	43.3	42.8	41.9	40.9	40.0	39.6	0.8
Rectum	19.4	19.0	19.3	20.0	19.2	19.2	18.4	18.6	18.4	-0.3
Pancreas	12.7	12.4	11.0	10.6	10.8	10.5	10.5	10.0	9.8	-1.0
Lung and bronchus	72.2	75.7	82.0	81.9	81.7	83.9	81.6	80.1	78.6	0.5
Prostate gland	62.3	68.8	78.4	86.4	90.1	101.9	104.9	110.2	128.5	3.5
Urinary bladder	27.2	28.6	31.3	31.0	32.1	33.5	32.7	31.9	31.6	1.0
Non-Hodgkin's lymphoma	10.2	11.4	12.6	15.9	16.6	18.2	17.9	18.1	19.0	3.9
Leukemia	14.3	14.1	14.5	14.2	14.2	13.8	13.5	13.5	12.3	-0.5
Black Male										
All sites	441.2	437.3	509.1	529.3	529.8	544.2	535.3	533.3	556.3	1.5
Oral cavity and pharynx	16.6	17.3	23.1	22.5	24.5	26.2	22.6	24.3	24.8	2.2
Esophagus	13.0	17.4	16.4	19.5	21.8	18.2	16.7	15.7	19.9	0.7
Stomach	26.1	19.9	21.4	18.4	18.4	20.7	20.0	18.4	17.6	-1.0
Colon and rectum	42.6	47.2	63.6	60.2	59.4	60.9	57.2	63.9	59.0	1.7
Colon	31.5	34.2	45.8	46.5	43.9	47.1	42.3	49.0	45.8	2.1
Rectum	11.1	13.0	17.7	13.7	15.5	13.8	14.9	14.9	13.1	0.8
Pancreas	15.8	15.4	17.6	19.8	16.2	16.0	16.9	12.7	15.0	-0.6
Lung and bronchus	105.1	101.2	131.2	131.7	134.3	123.7	125.8	121.0	116.0	1.3

Prostate gland	106.4	111.2	125.7	131.8	130.8	144.9	144.3	144.2	163.6	2.2
Urinary bladder	10.7	13.7	14.5	16.0	17.4	17.4	14.1	13.9	14.8	1.1
Non-Hodgkin's lymphoma	9.0	7.1	9.3	9.9	10.9	9.3	13.0	11.3	13.6	3.4
Leukemia	12.0	12.5	13.0	12.9	10.5	13.7	10.7	12.9	10.4	-0.2
White Female										
All sites	293.7	309.7	309.9	341.4	339.5	350.2	346.5	344.3	348.1	0.9
Colon and rectum	41.6	42.9	44.6	45.8	42.9	41.0	40.0	40.7	39.7	-0.3
Colon	30.2	30.8	32.9	33.8	32.1	30.1	29.3	29.9	29.7	-0.2
Rectum	11.4	12.0	11.8	11.9	10.8	10.9	10.7	10.8	10.0	-0.6
Pancreas	7.4	7.1	7.3	8.1	7.8	7.5	7.6	7.4	7.6	0.2
Lung and bronchus	17.8	21.9	28.3	35.9	37.7	39.6	41.4	40.6	41.5	4.9
Melanoma of skin	5.8	6.9	9.1	10.2	10.6	11.0	10.3	10.7	10.4	3.5
Breast	83.9	89.5	87.1	106.1	108.7	116.7	113.3	109.1	112.7	1.8
Cervix uteri	12.8	11.1	9.1	7.6	8.0	7.4	7.9	8.2	8.3	-2.6
Corpus uteri	29.4	33.7	25.3	23.1	22.3	22.6	21.3	22.0	22.7	-2.5
Ovary	14.6	14.4	13.9	15.0	13.5	14.6	15.5	16.0	15.7	0.4
Non-Hodgkin's lymphoma	7.5	8.4	9.2	11.3	11.1	11.4	12.1	11.7	12.4	2.8
Black Female										
All sites	282.8	296.0	304.3	322.7	328.2	326.2	334.4	320.5	334.4	1.0
Colon and rectum	41.1	43.4	49.4	45.8	47.2	47.8	45.9	44.4	48.8	0.9
Colon	29.5	32.8	40.9	36.0	36.7	37.1	36.4	34.1	38.3	1.3
Rectum	11.6	10.6	8.5	9.9	10.5	10.7	9.5	10.2	10.5	-0.0
Pancreas	11.6	11.8	13.0	11.3	13.0	14.8	14.2	11.1	10.6	0.5
Lung and bronchus	20.9	20.6	34.0	40.8	43.3	38.9	42.6	45.0	45.3	4.9
Breast	68.8	78.3	74.0	92.2	93.8	90.3	97.7	87.8	95.8	1.9
Cervix uteri	29.7	27.9	19.0	15.9	15.2	15.0	15.3	12.9	13.3	-4.5
Corpus uteri	15.0	17.2	14.1	15.1	14.2	13.8	14.0	16.5	14.5	-0.2
Ovary	10.5	10.1	10.0	10.0	9.1	10.0	10.6	10.7	10.4	0.2
Non-Hodgkin's lymphoma	5.5	4.1	6.2	6.8	6.8	8.0	7.2	7.8	8.5	3.9

[1]The estimated annual percent change has been calculated by fitting a linear regression model to the natural logarithm of the yearly rates from 1973–90.

[2]Age adjusted by the direct method to the 1970 U.S. population.

Source: National Cancer Institute, National Institutes of Health, Cancer Statistics Review, 1973–1990. NIH Pub. No. 93-2789. U.S. Department of Health and Human Services. Public Health Service. Bethesda, MD, 1993.

Table 2
Five-Year Relative Survival Rates by Race and Gender

Data are based on the Surveillance, Epidemiology, and End Results Program's population-based registries in Atlanta, Detroit, Seattle-Puget Sound, San Francisco-Oakland, Connecticut, Iowa, New Mexico, Utah, and Hawaii.

Sex and Site	All Races				White				Black			
	1974–76	1977–79	1980–82	1983–89	1974–76	1977–79	1980–82	1983–89	1974–76	1977–79	1980–82	1983–89
	Percent of patients											
Male												
All sites	40.9	43.0	44.9	47.8	42.0	44.3	46.3	49.6	31.2	32.1	33.9	34.4
Oral cavity and pharynx	52.3	51.1	50.7	49.5	54.5	53.4	54.0	52.4	30.8	30.8	25.5	27.4
Esophagus	3.5	4.7	6.0	8.2	4.2	5.6	6.7	9.2	2.1	2.4	4.6	6.3
Stomach	13.9	15.3	16.2	16.2	13.1	14.4	15.1	15.4	15.6	14.6	18.3	15.5
Colon	49.5	51.4	55.3	60.1	49.9	51.8	55.7	61.2	43.8	45.1	46.7	47.9
Rectum	47.4	48.7	50.1	56.3	47.8	49.8	51.2	57.3	34.1	38.0	36.1	42.8
Pancreas	2.9	2.2	2.8	2.6	3.2	2.2	2.7	2.3	1.2	2.8	3.7	4.4
Lung and bronchus	11.1	11.8	12.0	11.8	11.1	12.0	12.1	11.9	11.0	9.0	10.9	10.4
Prostate gland	66.7	70.8	73.1	77.6	67.7	71.9	74.2	79.4	57.8	62.1	64.2	64.4
Urinary bladder	73.7	76.3	79.1	81.0	74.5	76.7	79.8	81.5	54.5	62.4	62.3	66.9
Non-Hodgkin's lymphoma	46.9	45.5	50.0	49.8	47.7	46.1	50.7	50.4	43.1	42.1	47.1	41.7
Leukemia	33.0	35.8	36.8	37.5	33.5	36.7	38.0	38.9	31.9	29.4	29.3	29.6
Female												
All sites	56.7	56.0	55.9	57.9	56.8	56.7	56.7	59.1	46.7	46.2	45.5	44.7
Colon	50.6	53.6	55.0	58.1	50.7	53.7	55.2	59.1	46.9	49.5	50.5	49.2
Rectum	49.4	50.8	53.9	57.0	51.4	51.4	54.6	57.7	49.3	38.5	40.3	47.5
Pancreas	2.1	2.6	3.4	3.9	2.1	2.3	3.0	3.7	3.1	4.8	5.9	5.1
Lung and bronchus	15.6	17.0	15.9	15.7	15.8	17.0	16.0	16.0	12.9	16.9	15.4	13.0
Melanoma of skin	84.7	85.8	87.5	88.4	84.8	86.1	87.5	88.5			—	73.3
Breast	74.3	74.5	76.1	79.3	74.9	75.2	76.9	80.5	62.8	62.5	65.6	64.1
Cervix uteri	68.5	67.8	66.8	66.8	69.3	68.9	67.5	69.1	63.4	61.9	60.3	57.0
Corpus uteri	87.8	84.9	81.4	82.9	88.7	86.2	82.7	84.6	60.6	57.8	53.8	55.5
Ovary	36.5	38.1	38.8	40.6	36.3	37.5	38.7	40.2	40.1	39.8	37.3	40.2
Non-Hodgkin's lymphoma	47.3	50.5	52.5	53.9	47.4	50.4	52.6	54.5	54.1	58.9	54.7	46.5

Notes: Rates are based on follow up of patients through 1990. The rate is the ratio of the observed survival rate for the patient group to the expected survival rate persons in the general population similar to the patient group with respect to age, sex, race, and calendar year of observation. It estimates the chance of surviving effects of cancer.

Source: National Cancer Institute, National Institutes of Health, Cancer Statistics Review, 1973–1989. NIH Pub. No. 92-2789. U.S. Department of Health and Human Services. Public Health Service. Bethesda, MD, 1992; National Cancer Institute, Division of Cancer Prevention and Control: Unpublished data.

Table 3

Leading Causes of Death among African Americans, 1990

Cause	Male	Female
1. Heart disease	36,038	38,073
2. Cancer	31,995	25,082
3. Homicide and legal intervention	9,981	2,163
4. Unintentional injuries	8,756	3,663
5. Cerebralvascular diseases	7,653	9,754
6. Human immunodefiency virus infection	6,097	1,633
7. Pneumonia and influenza	4,161	3,402
8. Chronic obstructive lung disease	3,628	2,027
9. Diabetes	3,049	5,065
10. Chronic liver disease	2,393	1,360
11. Nephritis, nephrotic syndrome, and neophrosis	1,806	2,049
12. Suicide	1,737	374
13. Septicemia	1,624	1,841
14. Atherosclerosis	563	817

Source: USDHHS. (1993). Health, United States. United States Department of Health and Human Services: Bethesda, MD.

Table 4
Use of Cancer Screening Tests by Race and Gender

Breast Exam*—Percentage of females who never had procedure vs. females who had procedure, by race and age, 1987.

	Females					
	Never Had Procedure (%)		Had Procedure (%)			
					For Screening Purposes	
Race/Age	Never Heard of	Heard of But Never Had	For Health Problem	1 Yr Ago	1–3 Yrs Ago	>3 Yrs Ago
All Races**	9.4	10.1	7.2	43.6	15.1	14.6
White (Non-Hispanic)**	7.9	9.1	7.8	43.5	15.8	15.8
40–49	5.6	5.4	11.0	47.5	15.3	15.2
50–59	5.1	6.2	8.6	46.5	19.6	14.0
60–69	7.6	11.0	6.3	42.8	14.9	17.4
70+	13.9	14.8	4.7	36.4	13.7	16.6
Black (Non-Hispanic)**	15.5	12.7	5.0	45.9	12.0	8.9
40–49	8.9	11.2	5.7	53.5	15.0	5.6
50–59	15.0	7.7	6.1	46.5	12.5	12.3
60–69	14.6	14.9	4.5	46.4	10.4	9.2
70+	30.2	20.6	2.4	29.4	7.4	10.1
Hispanic**	13.4	14.7	4.0	45.0	11.7	11.2
40–49	12.5	9.6	4.8	52.1	12.9	8.2
50–59	8.5	20.4	5.4	50.8	8.3	6.5
60–69	14.4	12.3	1.5	36.4	13.9	21.5
70+	25.7	21.0	2.2	24.6	12.2	14.3

*Estimates are weighted to reflect U.S. Census population estimates for 1987.
**Females ages 40 or older.
Note: Data based on household interviews of the civilian noninstitutionalized population.
Source: Department of Health and Human Services, "Cancer Statistics Review 1973–1986," National Institutes of Health Pub. No. 89-2789, May 1989, Table II-25, p. II.52.

Table 5

Use of Cancer Screening Tests by Race and Gender

Mammography*—Percentage of females who never had procedure vs. females who had procedure, by race and age, 1987.

	Females					
	Never Had Procedure (%)		For Health Problem	Had Procedure (%)		
					For Screening Purposes	
Race/Age	Never Heard of	Heard of But Never Had		<= 1 Yr Ago	>1–3 Yrs Ago	>3 Yrs Ago
All Races**	15.6	47.5	6.6	16.6	6.4	7.3
White (Non-Hispanic)**	12.2	48.9	7.0	17.4	6.9	7.6
40–49	8.3	49.4	9.8	18.4	7.2	6.9
50–59	6.9	46.8	8.0	20.8	7.4	10.0
60–69	10.3	51.1	5.7	17.7	7.5	7.6
70+	23.7	48.1	4.1	12.8	5.3	5.9
Black (Non-Hispanic)**	29.4	40.9	5.6	14.2	3.9	5.9
40–49	18.1	45.9	10.7	12.4	4.5	8.3
50–59	25.4	44.5	2.9	18.6	4.3	4.4
60–69	35.3	36.4	4.5	17.1	3.3	3.5
70+	52.0	30.4	0.4	8.2	3.0	6.0
Hispanic**	31.6	42.2	3.1	12.9	3.1	7.1
40–49	24.2	52.3	3.2	11.6	1.8	6.9
50–59	30.1	32.9	4.2	17.5	7.0	8.3
60–69	30.3	45.2	3.2	10.4	2.1	8.7
70+	57.6	29.1	0.0	10.5	2.1	2.8

*Estimates are weighted to reflect U.S. Census population estimates for 1987.

**Females ages 40 or older.

Note: Data based on household interviews of the civilian noninstitutionalized population.

Source: Department of Health and Human Services, "Cancer Statistics Review 1973–1986," National Institutes of Health Pub. No. 89-2789, May 1989, Table II-26, p. II.53.

Table 6
Use of Cancer Screening Tests by Race and Gender

Pap Smears*—Percentage of females who never had procedure vs. females who had procedure, by race and age, 1987.

Race/Age	Never Had Procedure (%)		For Health Problem	Had Procedure (%)		
	Never Heard of	Heard of But Never Had		For Screening Purposes		
				<= 1 Yr Ago	>1–3 Yrs Ago	>3 Yrs Ago
All Races**	4.0	7.3	7.8	48.0	17.0	15.8
White (Non-Hispanic)**	2.1	6.9	7.6	47.9	17.8	17.7
18–29	2.6	11.3	10.1	59.4	13.8	2.9
30–39	0.6	2.0	9.6	55.5	20.5	11.7
40–49	2.0	2.3	7.1	49.3	18.5	20.9
50–59	0.6	3.6	6.9	43.7	21.4	23.9
60–69	1.7	6.0	5.2	38.0	18.4	30.6
70+	5.9	16.7	3.2	25.6	16.1	32.5
Black (Non-Hispanic)**	4.1	7.8	10.6	52.8	15.4	9.2
18–29	3.4	8.4	14.0	62.5	8.8	2.9
30–39	1.4	2.5	11.7	59.6	19.5	5.3
40–49	0.5	2.2	10.9	59.9	18.3	8.2
50–59	4.5	6.2	7.5	41.4	21.4	18.9
60–69	5.1	16.8	7.0	38.2	15.9	17.0
70+	19.7	23.7	3.2	17.2	13.7	22.6
Hispanic**	15.1	9.6	7.4	44.8	12.9	10.3
18–29	16.0	14.5	9.8	48.4	8.9	2.3
30–39	10.0	3.4	6.9	53.2	16.7	9.8
40–49	10.3	3.3	9.3	46.9	19.2	10.9
50–59	19.7	10.7	4.3	38.4	10.9	16.0
60–69	19.4	9.9	1.5	26.9	15.0	27.3
70+	26.8	16.2	1.8	19.9	8.0	27.4

*Estimates are weighted to reflect U.S. Census population estimates for 1987.

**Females ages 18 or older.

Source: Department of Health and Human Services, "Cancer Statistics Review 1973–1986," National Institutes of Health Pub. No. 89-2789, May 1989, Table II–24, p. II.51.

Table 7

Use of Cancer Screening Tests by Race and Gender

Proctoscopy*—Percentage of females who never had procedure vs. females who had procedure, by race and age, 1987.

Race/Age	Never Had Procedure (%)		For Health Problem	Had Procedure (%) For Screening Purposes		
	Never Heard of	Heard of But Never Had		<= 1 Yr Ago	>1–3 Yrs Ago	>3 Yrs Ago
All Races**	32.5	47.4	4.8	2.5	2.2	10.7
White (Non-Hispanic)**	28.1	49.6	5.4	2.7	2.4	11.8
40–49	23.3	63.1	3.2	1.1	0.9	8.3
50–59	23.1	51.8	6.6	2.7	2.7	13.2
60–69	26.9	46.3	6.7	4.0	3.1	13.1
70+	40.0	34.5	5.4	3.6	3.1	13.3
Black (Non-Hispanic)**	50.4	38.4	2.2	1.7	1.6	5.7
40–49	45.5	44.7	2.2	1.9	0.5	5.3
50–59	44.5	41.0	2.8	0.7	1.5	9.5
60–69	50.9	36.5	2.3	2.8	4.0	3.5
70+	69.2	23.6	0.9	1.5	1.5	3.3
Hispanic**	55.6	33.8	1.9	0.8	1.2	6.8
40–49	53.6	39.3	0.5	16.7	2.2	4.5
50–59	53.7	34.0	3.8	1.1	1.0	6.4
60–69	55.3	31.0	1.4	2.2	1.0	10.1
70+	66.2	21.2	2.4	0.0	1.0	9.2

*Estimates are weighted to reflect U.S. Census population estimates for 1987.

**Members of the referenced population ages 40 or older.

Note: Data based on household interviews of the civilian noninstitutionalized population.

Source: Department of Health and Human Services, "Cancer Statistics Review 1973–1986," National Institutes of Health Pub. No. 89-2789, May 1989, Table II–29, p. II.59.

Table 8
Use of Cancer Screening Tests by Race and Gender

Digital Rectal Exam*—Percentage of males who never had procedure vs. males who had procedure, by race and age, 1987.

Race/Age	Never Had Procedure (%)		Had Procedure (%)			
					For Screening Purposes	
	Never Heard of	Heard of But Never Had	For Health Problem	≤ 1 Yr Ago	>1–3 Yrs Ago	>3 Yrs Ago
All Races**	22.8	19.1	10.9	17.1	10.4	19.6
White (Non-Hispanic)**	20.2	19.0	11.0	18.1	11.3	20.4
40–49	19.1	26.6	8.0	11.9	13.0	21.4
50–59	23.6	18.3	9.7	17.9	10.1	20.4
60–69	15.8	13.7	15.9	22.2	12.5	19.9
70+	22.9	14.0	11.8	23.4	8.6	19.4
Black (Non-Hispanic)**	38.2	16.4	10.8	15.7	5.9	13.0
40–49	33.3	22.3	6.6	15.0	6.9	15.8
50–59	43.6	15.8	8.6	9.9	6.3	15.7
60–69	31.4	9.8	22.2	21.3	5.7	9.7
70+	49.7	14.1	7.5	18.0	3.1	7.6
Hispanic**	29.3	28.5	10.5	8.4	7.2	16.1
40–49	32.0	30.0	6.6	7.4	5.1	18.8
50–59	27.0	29.5	12.2	8.7	11.8	10.9
60–69	20.2	30.0	18.9	6.7	9.1	15.2
70+	40.1	17.3	7.4	13.8	9.1	21.3

*Estimates are weighted to reflect U.S. Census population estimates for 1987.
**Members of the referenced population ages 40 or older.
Note: Data based on household interviews of the civilian noninstitutionalized population.
Source: Department of Health and Human Services, "Cancer Statistics Review 1973–1986," National Institutes of Health Pub. No. 89-2789, May 1989, Table II-27, p. II.54.

Table 9

Use of Cancer Screening Tests by Race and Gender

Digital Rectal Exam*—Percentage of females who never had procedure vs. females who had procedure, by race and age, 1987.

| | Never Had Procedure (%) | | For Health Problem | Had Procedure (%) | | |
| | Never Heard of | Heard of But Never Had | | For Screening Purposes | | |
Race/Age				≤ 1 Yr Ago	>1–3 Yrs Ago	>3 Yrs Ago
All Races**	20.1	23.0	7.0	23.6	9.4	16.9
White (Non-Hispanic)**	17.2	22.9	7.3	24.8	10.0	17.8
40–49	16.5	25.3	5.3	27.1	9.5	16.3
50–59	13.1	22.2	9.8	26.3	10.9	17.8
60–69	14.3	22.3	7.2	26.8	9.5	20.0
70+	25.0	21.3	7.2	18.6	10.2	17.6
Black (Non-Hispanic)**	31.4	20.6	6.7	21.9	5.8	13.6
40–49	26.2	21.3	6.9	27.4	4.2	14.0
50–59	30.1	19.2	4.2	19.8	7.9	18.8
60–69	27.7	21.8	11.1	23.2	7.0	9.1
70+	48.3	20.1	4.9	12.3	4.7	9.8
Hispanic**	31.5	28.5	5.3	15.1	6.9	12.7
40–49	32.1	32.3	5.1	13.4	5.5	11.6
50–59	32.5	30.8	3.5	20.3	3.9	9.1
60–69	23.5	23.0	7.5	12.3	11.5	22.2
70+	40.5	20.9	6.5	12.7	10.5	8.8

*Estimates are weighted to reflect U.S. Census population estimates for 1987.

**Members of the referenced population ages 40 or older.

Note: Data based on household interviews of the civilian noninstitutionalized population.

Source: Department of Health and Human Services, "Cancer Statistics Review 1973–1986," National Institutes of Health Pub. No. 89-2789, May 1989, Table II-27, p. II.55.

Table 10
Use of Cancer Screening Tests by Race and Gender

Blood Stool Tests* — Percentage of males who never had procedure vs. males who had procedure, by race and age, 1987.

| Race/Age | Never Had Procedure (%) | | Had Procedure (%) | | | |
| | Never Heard of | Heard of But Never Had | For Health Problem | For Screening Purposes | | |
				<1 Yr Ago	<= 1-3 Yrs Ago	>3 Yrs Ago
All Races**	19.1	44.8	5.9	11.6	7.3	11.4
White (Non-Hispanic)**	15.2	47.1	6.1	12.4	7.7	11.4
40–49	13.4	54.2	4.5	8.3	7.8	11.8
50–59	14.1	49.0	6.5	13.0	7.0	10.3
60–69	11.8	43.3	7.6	14.9	9.7	12.7
70+	23.7	37.7	6.2	15.4	6.1	10.9
Black (Non-Hispanic)**	38.3	34.3	5.6	6.6	5.6	9.7
40–49	31.5	47.1	3.0	5.3	4.8	8.3
50–59	44.0	28.7	3.8	4.7	5.4	13.5
60–69	35.0	27.2	11.4	9.8	7.2	9.6
70+	48.4	25.2	5.8	7.9	5.5	7.2
Hispanic**	39.7	33.4	4.9	6.6	3.0	12.4
40–49	39.1	36.7	5.6	4.6	4.1	9.9
50–59	30.9	29.2	7.1	13.1	3.0	16.8
60–69	42.8	39.0	2.7	2.2	2.4	10.9
70+	60.9	23.8	0.0	3.0	2.4	12.2

*Estimates are weighted to reflect U.S. Census population estimates for 1987.

**Members of the referenced population ages 40 or older.

Note: Data based on household interviews of the civilian noninstitutionalized population.

Source: Department of Health and Human Services, "Cancer Statistics Review 1973–1986," National Institutes of Health Pub. No. 89-2789, May 1989, Table II-28, p. II.56.

Table 11
Use of Cancer Screening Tests by Race and Gender

Blood Stool Tests*—Percentage of females who never had procedure vs. females who had procedure, by race and age, 1987.

| | Never Had Procedure (%) | | | Had Procedure (%) | | |
| | | | | For Screening Purposes | | |
Race/Age	Never Heard of	Heard of But Never Had	For Health Problem	<= 1 Yr Ago	>1–3 Yrs Ago	>3 Yrs Ago
All Races**	15.0	48.7	6.1	14.6	6.0	9.6
White (Non-Hispanic)**	12.0	49.9	6.5	15.4	6.3	9.9
40–49	10.4	62.3	4.2	10.1	4.5	8.5
50–59	9.0	49.1	8.7	16.2	6.4	10.5
60–69	9.0	45.2	6.7	20.6	7.9	10.6
70+	20.0	40.4	6.7	16.0	6.7	10.2
Black (Non-Hispanic)**	24.4	44.4	4.7	12.5	4.8	9.1
40–49	17.5	54.5	3.6	12.1	2.8	9.5
50–59	24.2	37.0	4.6	16.3	4.7	13.3
60–69	21.4	44.8	9.0	11.4	8.6	4.8
70+	42.1	34.5	2.4	8.7	5.0	7.2
Hispanic**	33.7	39.9	4.5	9.4	5.2	7.4
40–49	34.8	42.5	4.0	8.9	6.4	3.3
50–59	32.5	37.4	4.1	10.6	4.2	11.3
60–69	27.8	41.4	4.5	11.0	3.6	11.7
70+	42.4	35.6	6.9	5.4	6.3	3.4

*Estimates are weighted to reflect U.S. Census population estimates for 1987.

**Members of the referenced population ages 40 or older.

Note: Data based on household interviews of the civilian noninstitutionalized population.

Source: Department of Health and Human Services, "Cancer Statistics Review 1973–1986," National Institutes of Health Pub. No. 89-2789, May 1989, Table II–28, p. II.57.

Table 12
Use of Cancer Screening Tests by Race and Gender

Proctoscopy*—Percentage of males who never had procedure vs. males who had procedure, by race and age, 1987.

Race/Age	Never Had Procedure (%)		Had Procedure (%)			
	Never Heard of	Heard of But Never Had	For Health Problem	For Screening Purposes		
				<= 1 Yr Ago	>1–3 Yrs Ago	>3 Yrs Ago
All Races**	35.2	42.4	5.5	3.2	3.1	10.7
White (Non-Hispanic)**	31.4	44.5	5.7	3.5	3.3	11.6
40–49	30.4	54.7	4.0	1.5	2.0	7.3
50–59	30.1	46.5	4.1	3.7	3.7	11.9
60–69	26.3	40.4	9.2	3.8	5.0	15.3
70+	40.9	30.3	6.6	5.8	2.8	13.5
Black (Non-Hispanic)**	56.6	29.5	3.8	2.1	3.1	4.8
40–49	49.4	38.4	1.7	3.0	3.8	3.7
50–59	59.6	30.9	2.7	0.4	1.8	4.7
60–69	54.0	26.4	7.5	3.8	2.4	5.9
70+	70.7	13.0	5.3	0.4	4.5	6.1
Hispanic**	51.1	35.0	5.5	0.8	1.3	6.3
40–49	53.5	34.4	5.1	0.0	1.2	5.8
50–59	50.7	30.6	6.9	2.0	1.5	8.3
60–69	44.6	43.3	7.6	1.0	1.5	3.4
70+	53.7	35.5	0.0	0.0	3.0	7.8

*Estimates are weighted to reflect U.S. Census population estimates for 1987.

**Members of the referenced population ages 40 or older.

Note: Data based on household interviews of the civilian noninstitutionalized population.

Source: Department of Health and Human Services. "Cancer Statistics Review 1973–1986," National Institutes of Health Pub. No. 89-2789, May 1989, Table II-29, p. II.58.

Table 13

Prevalence of Cigarette Smoking by Race and Gender, 1990

Percent of persons 18 years of age and over who currently smoked cigarettes, by sex, age, and selected characteristics: United States, 1990
Data are based on household interviews of the civilian noninstitutionalized population.

Characteristic	Both Sexes 18 Years and Over	Male					Female				
		Total	18–29 Years	30–44 Years	45–64 Years	65 Years and Over	Total	18–29 Years	30–44 Years	45–64 Years	65 Years and Over
All persons[1]	25.5	28.4	28.6	33.6	29.3	14.6	22.8	25.3	25.8	24.8	11.5
Education Level											
Less than 12 years	31.8	37.3	44.6	54.0	39.4	17.4	27.1	40.9	40.3	29.9	10.9
12 years	29.6	33.5	33.4	40.9	32.3	16.2	26.5	29.8	32.1	25.5	11.9
More than 12 years	18.3	20.0	16.1	23.9	21.5	8.7	16.6	14.5	17.2	20.5	11.8
13–15 years	23.0	26.2	20.4	34.3	27.6	8.9	20.2	17.3	23.5	22.8	13.0
16 years or more	13.5	14.5	8.8	16.0	17.6	8.6	12.3	9.3	11.1	18.2	10.2
Income											
Less than $10,000	31.6	37.3	30.6	59.7	47.0	21.1	28.6	31.9	46.6	33.2	13.2
$10,000–$19,999	29.8	34.1	35.8	44.7	40.7	16.4	26.3	31.9	36.5	26.1	12.2
$20,000–$34,999	26.9	30.3	30.6	37.0	30.5	13.0	23.5	22.3	27.1	26.5	12.1
$35,000–$49,999	23.4	25.5	22.8	28.4	27.4	10.9	21.0	19.7	22.4	22.5	10.2
$50,000 or more	19.3	21.3	20.6	24.1	20.7	10.1	17.2	17.7	16.2	19.0	12.3
Race											
White	25.6	28.0	29.1	33.0	28.7	13.7	23.4	27.1	26.1	25.4	11.5
Black	26.2	32.5	26.7	38.8	36.7	21.5	21.2	17.9	27.2	22.6	11.1
Hispanic Origin											
Hispanic	23.0	30.9	28.5	35.9	30.2	19.4	16.3	15.7	18.6	18.1	*5.1
Non-Hispanic	25.7	28.2	28.6	33.4	29.3	14.4	23.4	26.7	26.6	25.3	11.7

Table 13 (continued)

Characteristic	Both Sexes 18 Years and Over	Male					Female				
		Total	18–29 Years	30–44 Years	45–64 Years	65 Years and Over	Total	18–29 Years	30–44 Years	45–64 Years	65 Years and Over
Geographic Region											
Northeast	23.9	26.8	28.0	31.1	26.7	15.0	21.3	25.9	24.6	22.2	10.3
Midwest	27.4	29.4	31.9	33.6	30.2	14.0	25.6	29.4	29.8	27.6	10.1
South	26.5	30.4	29.4	35.9	32.5	16.4	22.9	24.9	25.4	25.7	12.2
West	23.2	25.6	24.1	32.1	25.9	11.6	20.9	20.9	23.2	22.6	13.5
Marital Status											
Currently married	24.6	27.1	32.2	31.5	27.0	12.6	22.1	27.6	23.1	21.9	10.5
Formerly married	30.3	41.1	43.9	49.3	44.4	23.8	25.9	44.3	37.9	33.5	12.4
Never married	24.3	26.7	25.4	32.6	28.8	12.7	21.3	20.2	28.0	23.2	*8.8
Employment Status											
Currently employed	26.9	29.2	28.1	31.8	27.9	16.3	24.2	24.5	24.6	24.5	15.5
Unemployed	38.8	45.8	43.1	53.1	43.5	*16.7	31.2	29.8	38.1	25.1	*6.4
Not in labor force	21.3	23.3	25.5	51.7	33.3	14.2	20.3	26.5	28.1	25.2	11.0

[1]Includes persons with unknown sociodemographic characteristics.
Note: Denominator for each cell excludes unknowns.

Table 14
Median Daily Nutrient Intake by Race and Gender*

Nutrient	Age	White (Non-Hispanic)		Black (Non-Hispanic)		Hispanic	
		Males	Females	Males	Females	Males	Females
% Fat	18+	38.6	39.0	38.4	39.5	34.4	36.2
	18–24	38.5	39.0	38.8	40.9	35.2	38.0
	25–34	38.5	39.6	38.8	40.5	34.3	36.5
	35–44	38.9	39.6	37.4	38.3	33.9	36.3
	45–64	38.8	38.9	38.0	37.9	34.2	35.1
	65+	38.3	37.9	38.3	37.8	34.9	33.5
Fiber (g)	18+	10.4	8.1	10.4	8.0	13.9	9.6
	18–24	11.1	7.0	11.5	8.4	15.3	9.5
	25–34	10.7	7.8	11.3	7.7	15.9	10.0
	35–44	9.7	7.8	9.8	7.7	12.2	9.9
	45–64	10.1	8.6	9.2	8.1	12.2	9.9
	65+	10.6	8.6	9.1	8.2	13.0	8.5
Fiber/1000 Kcal	18+	5.5	6.4	5.3	5.8	6.5	6.7
	18–24	4.5	4.9	5.0	4.7	5.5	5.8
	25–34	5.0	5.5	4.9	5.0	6.4	6.4
	35–44	5.3	6.2	5.2	6.0	6.5	7.0
	45–64	5.9	7.2	5.7	6.9	7.1	7.8
	65+	7.1	8.0	6.3	7.3	8.0	7.7

By race, persons 18 years of age or older

Nutrient	All Races	White & Blacks (Non-Hispanic)	Hispanic
%Fat	38.5	38.8	35.4
Fiber (g)	9.2	9.1	11.5
Fiber/1000 Kcal	5.9	5.9	6.7

*Estimates are weighted to reflect U.S. Census population estimates for 1987. Source: Department of Health and Human Services, "Cancer Statistics Review 1973–1986," National Institutes of Health Pub. No. 89-2789, May 1989, Table II-16, p. II.44.

Table 15
Median Intake Frequency per Week for
Selected Foods by Race and Gender*

Food	White		Black		Hispanic	
	Male	Female	Male	Female	Male	Female
High-fiber bread or cereal	3.0	3.0	0.5	1.0	1.0	1.0
All fruit	3.0	3.9	2.5	3.2	3.4	4.2
Fruit and juice	7.5	9.0	8.0	9.0	9.1	10.2
Dried legumes, chili	0.7	0.5	1.0	0.5	2.0	1.0
Garden vegetabl˙ ˙	4.9	5.4	5.0	5.2	6.2	7.0
Potatoes	4.0	3.0	3.0	2.7	3.2	3.0
Salad	2.0	3.0	1.0	1.2	2.0	3.0
Hamburger, beef, pork	3.3	2.5	3.2	2.7	4.0	3.2
Chicken and fish	1.6	1.7	3.0	2.9	2.3	2.0
Bacon, sausage, hot dogs, lunch meats	3.5	2.1	5.0	3.6	3.4	2.2
Beer, wine, liquors	1.9	0.2	1.3	0.0	2.6	0.1

*Estimates are weighted to reflect U.S. Census population estimates for 1987.
Source: National Health Interview Survey, 1987.

Table 16
Characteristics of African American Foods and Food Choices

Protein Foods

Meat:	Beef, pork and ham, sausage, pig's feet, ears, etc., bacon, luncheon meats, organ meats
Poultry:	Chicken, turkey
Fish:	Catfish, perch, red snapper, tuna, salmon, sardines, shrimp
Eggs:	Fried
Legumes:	Kidney beans, red beans, pinto beans, black-eyed peas
Nuts:	Peanuts, peanut butter

Milk and Milk Products

Milk:	Fluid, evaporated milk in coffee, buttermilk
Cheese:	Cheddar, cottage
Ice cream	

Grain Products

Rice, cornbread, hominy grits, biscuits, white bread, dry cereal, cooked cereal, macaroni, spaghetti, crackers

Vegetables

Broccoli, cabbage, carrots, corn, green beans, greens (mustards, collards, kale, spinach, turnips), lima beans, okra, peas, potatoes, pumpkins, sweet potatoes, tomatoes, yams

Fruit

Apples, bananas, grapefruit, grapes, nectarines, oranges, plums, tangerines, watermelon

Other

Salt pork, fruit drinks, carbonated beverages, gravies

Table 17
Alcohol Consumption by Race, 1990

Data are based on household interviews of the civilian noninstitutionalized population.

Characteristic	Both Sexes 18 Years and Over	Male					Female				
		Total	18–29 Years	30–44 Years	45–64 Years	65 Years and Over	Total	18–29 Years	30–44 Years	45–64 Years	65 Years and Over
All persons[1]	60.7	71.8	75.6	78.3	68.4	55.6	50.7	58.5	58.2	47.6	31.3
Education Level											
Less than 12 years	42.6	57.8	67.2	71.2	54.0	44.2	29.2	44.4	39.2	28.5	16.6
12 years	59.8	71.9	74.6	77.7	67.3	58.7	50.3	55.8	56.5	46.4	36.4
More than 12 years	71.0	78.5	80.6	80.5	77.1	68.5	63.3	67.0	64.1	63.1	51.2
13–15 years	68.0	76.2	79.1	78.2	74.0	61.5	60.8	64.4	61.7	59.7	49.2
16 years or more	74.2	80.6	83.3	82.3	79.1	73.5	66.4	71.8	66.4	66.5	53.9
Income											
Less than $10,000	44.9	60.8	72.9	70.8	51.5	36.6	36.3	54.4	46.0	29.5	17.5
$10,000–$19,999	51.6	63.3	71.9	72.4	55.7	49.4	42.1	53.2	49.7	36.7	29.1
$20,000–$34,999	61.7	72.2	75.0	76.7	67.0	63.7	51.7	58.6	56.2	44.1	40.5
$35,000–$49,999	68.2	75.0	77.5	78.4	70.1	64.2	60.6	66.3	62.4	53.7	55.7
$50,000 or more	76.0	83.6	83.2	87.1	81.2	77.3	67.9	71.2	69.9	65.0	58.4
Race											
White	63.1	73.6	78.5	80.1	70.2	56.9	53.6	63.3	61.7	50.4	33.0
Black	46.4	62.7	64.8	71.3	57.9	39.8	33.3	36.0	40.5	30.0	15.0
Hispanic Origin											
Hispanic	52.3	69.2	66.1	76.8	66.1	54.3	37.9	41.7	42.2	29.5	23.5
Non-Hispanic	61.4	72.0	76.8	78.5	68.5	55.7	51.8	60.8	59.7	49.0	31.6
Geographic Region											
Northeast	65.6	75.9	77.3	82.3	73.9	62.2	56.5	64.8	63.2	56.9	36.6
Midwest	66.4	77.1	84.1	81.9	73.4	60.2	56.5	67.0	65.4	52.7	32.6

South	52.2	65.0	69.9	74.1	59.8	45.0	40.9	49.8	49.1	35.3	22.6
West	63.2	72.6	73.3	77.2	71.0	62.0	54.5	58.0	59.5	53.0	39.9
Marital Status											
Currently married	61.9	71.7	79.5	77.9	68.1	57.3	52.1	57.5	57.4	48.2	36.1
Formerly married	51.2	72.2	85.0	83.9	72.8	50.2	42.7	62.1	63.2	46.0	27.5
Never married	64.9	72.0	72.5	76.4	61.5	47.2	56.2	58.9	56.0	47.2	32.6
Employment Status											
Currently employed	68.3	76.0	77.5	79.2	71.4	62.1	59.0	64.1	60.9	52.1	44.7
Unemployed	65.5	73.7	76.8	74.6	68.3	*57.7	56.5	56.6	58.3	51.9	62.8
Not in labor force	44.6	56.8	63.0	66.4	55.3	54.2	38.7	45.2	49.6	40.9	29.5

[1]Includes persons with unknown sociodemographic characteristics.

Note: Denominator for each cell excludes unknowns.

Table 18

Poverty Levels by Race, Age, and Region

Data are based on household interviews of the civilian noninstitutionalized population.

Selected Characteristics, Race, and Hispanic Origin	1973	1980¹	1985	1986	1987	1988	1989	1990	1991
	Percent below Poverty								
All persons									
All races	11.1	13.0	14.0	13.6	13.4	13.0	12.8	13.5	14.2
White	8.4	10.2	11.4	11.0	10.4	10.1	10.0	10.7	11.3
Black	31.4	32.5	31.3	31.1	32.4	31.3	30.7	31.9	32.7
Hispanic	21.9	25.7	29.0	27.3	28.0	26.7	26.2	28.1	28.7
Related children under 18 years of age in families									
All races	14.2	17.9	20.1	19.8	19.7	19.0	19.0	19.9	21.1
White	9.7	13.4	15.6	15.3	14.7	14.0	14.1	15.1	16.1
Black	40.6	42.1	43.1	42.7	44.4	42.8	43.2	44.2	45.6
Hispanic	27.8	33.0	39.6	37.1	38.9	37.3	35.5	37.7	39.8
Families with female householder, no husband present, and children under 18 years of age									
All races	43.2	42.9	45.4	46.0	45.5	44.7	42.8	44.5	47.1
White	35.2	35.9	38.7	39.8	38.3	38.2	36.1	37.9	39.6
Black	58.8	56.0	58.9	58.0	58.6	56.2	53.9	56.1	60.5
Hispanic	—	57.3	64.0	59.5	60.9	59.2	57.9	58.2	60.1
All persons	Number below Poverty in Thousands								
All races	22,973	29,272	33,064	32,370	32,221	31,745	31,528	33,585	35,708
White	15,142	19,699	22,860	22,183	21,195	20,715	20,785	22,326	23,747

Black	7,388	8,579	8,926	8,983	9,520	9,356	9,302	9,837	10,242
Hispanic	2,366	3,491	5,236	5,117	5,422	5,357	5,430	6,006	6,339
Related children under 18 years of age in families									
All races	9,453	11,114	12,483	12,257	12,275	11,935	12,001	12,715	13,658
White	5,462	6,817	7,838	7,714	7,398	7,095	7,164	7,696	8,316
Black	3,822	3,906	4,057	4,037	4,234	4,148	4,257	4,412	4,637
Hispanic	1,364	1,718	2,512	2,413	2,606	2,576	2,496	2,750	2,977
Families with female householder, no husband present, and children under 18 years of age									
All races	1,987	2,703	3,131	3,264	3,281	3,294	3,190	3,426	3,767
White	1,053	1,433	1,730	1,812	1,742	1,740	1,671	1,814	1,969
Black	905	1,217	1,336	1,384	1,437	1,452	1,415	1,513	1,676
Hispanic	—	288	493	489	527	510	491	536	584

[1]Data for Hispanic families with female householder, no husband present, and children under 18 years are for 1979.

Notes: The race groups, white and black, include persons of both Hispanic and non-Hispanic origin. Conversely, persons of Hispanic origin may be of any race. Some numbers in this table have been revised and differ from previous editions of Health, United States.

Source: U.S. Bureau of the Census: Poverty in the United States 1991. Current Population Reports, Series P-60, No. 181, Washington. U.S. Government Printing Office, Aug. 1992.

Chapter Three

Home Grown Violence: The Abuse of African American Children

Pamela V. Hammond

A s violence becomes the topic of an increasing number of news reports, articles, books, and other media, emphasis must be placed on the effects of this phenomenon on the health and safety of children and the resulting social problems that affect children and their families. The crime of child abuse and neglect is one of the most devastating social problems that exists in a violent society. Child abuse and neglect affects the health of all our children and, thereby, affects the health of the total community.

Literature relating to the prevalence and patterns of child abuse and neglect, specifically in the African American community, is lacking both in numbers and depth. There is a need for an increased awareness among families, school officials, and other community leaders of the long lasting and cyclic nature of this crime so devastating to future generations. Such an awareness would serve to increase the community's involvement in the prevention, identification, and treatment of child abuse and neglect, and decrease many of the prevailing myths surrounding it—myths that serve to obscure the complexity and origin of the problems themselves.

Gelles and Cornell (1990) outline seven myths related directly to child abuse and neglect: (1) family violence is rare, (2) family violence is confined to mentally disturbed or sick people, (3) family violence is confined to the lower class, (4) family violence occurs in all groups, (5) children who are abused will grow up to be child abusers, (6) alcohol and drug abuse are the real causes of violence in the home, and (7) violence and love do not coexist in families.

According to Gelles and Cornell (1990), these myths hinder progress toward public awareness of family violence and must be dispelled before professionals can provide the level of assistance necessary to end the violence. Child abuse and neglect reporting patterns are influenced greatly by the myths, values, and beliefs of mandatory reporters, as well as friends, neighbors, and relatives.

In this chapter, I will focus on the violence experienced by African American children, generally at the hands of their parents or other caregivers. By this, I do not intend to imply that child abuse and neglect is a problem peculiar to African Americans. The act of inflicting violence on the young crosses all boundaries of race, age, and socioeconomic status.

HISTORICAL AND LEGISLATIVE PERSPECTIVE

She was called "Little Mary Ellen." Her legal name was Mary Ellen Wilson as found in the official records of the court of New York in 1874. Her only crime was that of being a child. Little Mary Ellen was involved in the first recorded case in which a court was used to protect a child. She was taken away from her mother on the grounds of child abuse after Henry Bergh persuaded a New York court to hear the case (*The New York Times,* April, 1874).

An interesting point to be made here is that Mr. Bergh was the founder and president of the Society for the Prevention of Cruelty to Animals (SPCA) at the time the plight of Little Mary Ellen became known to him. The SPCA was founded in 1866, eight years before the founding of the Society for the Prevention of Cruelty to Children, eight years before the world knew of "Little Mary Ellen" whose case led to the formation of the Society for Prevention of Cruelty to Children (*The New York Times,* December, 1874). The purpose of this society was to enforce legally and energetically the existing laws and to secure conviction and punishment of every violation of any of the related laws. Yes, laws against ill treatment, although not specifically of children, did exist prior to deliberation on Mary Ellen's case. Enforcement of those laws, whether for the benefit of children or adults, is another matter, requiring that the crime be committed, a victim found, a perpetrator charged, and a verdict attained. Enforcement, we must remember, and especially in regard to laws against ill treatment, usually does not prevent the crime—it follows it.

Cruelty to children has been recorded throughout history. Even in our own century, children with defects and female babies are killed in some societies, while in others it is expected that a man may do with his property (wife and children) as he sees fit. Thanks to the bravery of Mary Ellen, U.S. courts finally said "enough." Despite the publicity and public outpour of feelings for Mary Ellen and disgust for her parents, it took 100 more years and many other like cases for the U.S. Congress to finally pass a law to found the agency, National Center on Child Abuse and Neglect, to coordinate programs related to child abuse.

Gelles and Cornell (1990) report that current public awareness of child abuse and neglect is a fairly new phenomenon prompted by three pivotal events of the 1960s: the publication of the benchmark article by Kempe et al. (1962) regarding the prevalence of physical abuse inflicted upon children by their parents; the recognition of child abuse and neglect by legislators which resulted in the passage of child abuse and neglect laws in all 50 states; and the involvement of the federal government in attempts to educate the public on the issues surrounding this national crime. The advent of public awareness of child abuse as a social problem affecting all segments of the community brought about measures to ensure that the crime was reported to the proper authorities by those individuals who came into contact with children as a result of professional involvement.

For its part, in 1974, Congress sought to ensure the protection of children by passing Public Law (PL) 93-247, the Child Abuse Prevention and Treatment Act. This law established the National Center on Child Abuse and Neglect which coordinates all federal programs related to child abuse and neglect. In addition to the establishment of the National Center on Child Abuse and Neglect, PL 93-247 provided funds to be appropriated to public nonprofit organizations for demonstration programs and projects designed to prevent, identify, and treat child abuse and neglect.

Within a year after the passing of PL 3-247, most states had passed laws for the protection of children. Each state, by virtue of the persons being required to report suspected child abuse and neglect, has indicated support of the notion that child abuse and neglect is a total community health problem. It also is a multiphasic problem in need of the attention of a variety of professionals and volunteers in order to provide adequate identification, treatment, and prevention (Sloan, 1983).

INCIDENCE IN THE AFRICAN AMERICAN COMMUNITY

Nationally, there were approximately 2.7 million children who were subjects of reports of abuse and neglect to social service agencies during 1991 (U.S. Bureau of the Census, 1993). Of the child abuse and neglect cases that were reported and investigated by child protective services, 838,232 were substantiated (determined to have sufficient evidence to conclude that abuse/neglect occurred or that a child was at risk). Neglect comprised the largest proportion (46%) of the cases with physical abuse at 24 percent, sexual abuse at 16 percent, and emotional abuse at 6 percent. Abused children 5 years and younger accounted for 39 percent (320,420) of the maltreated population. McCurdy and Daro (1994) found that much of the increase in the numbers of children reported can be attributed to change in public attitude and awareness, state reporting patterns, and family stress related to economics. Table 1 illustrates the race/ethnic group characteristics of child victims in 1991.

In 1991, there were 218,026 (26.7%) African American victims of child abuse and neglect. This figure was up 20,626 cases over the 1990 statistics (197,400/25.5%). These statistics indicate that a crisis is exploding in African American communities. African Americans, we must recall, comprised only 12 percent of the total U.S. population in 1990 (U.S. Bureau of the Census, 1993).

Hampton (1987) in a study of 17,645 cases of child abuse found that differences do exist among African Americans, whites, and Hispanics in cases of physical abuse. Specifically, the groups differed in regard to family income, age of victim, perpetrator, and type and severity of abuse. African American children were found to be assaulted more in the early school years, lived in urban areas, had mothers who dropped out of school, were less likely to

Table 1
Race/Ethnic Characteristics of Child Abuse and Neglect Victims Substantiated, 1991

	Number	Percent
White	453,955	55.5
Black (African American)	218,026	26.7
Asian and Pacific Islander	6,564	0.8
American Indian, Eskimo, and Aleut	10,875	1.3
Other Races	13,005	1.6
Hispanic Origin	78,025	9.5
Unknown	37,268	4.6

Source: U.S. Bureau of the Census, (1993). *Statistical abstract of the United States: 1993* (113th ed.). Washington, DC.

be classified as victims of emotional injury, and lived in families with more children and more victims.

African American children (52%) were more likely than white (27.4%) or Hispanic children (44.4%) to suffer injuries inflicted by weapons (knife, gun, stick, or cord) (Hampton, 1987). In addition, African American children were more likely to be sexually abused in their own homes or neighborhoods by persons known to them such as stepfathers, mothers, boyfriends, foster fathers, babysitters, neighbors, or friends (Wyatt, 1985). Furthermore, child abuse cases among African American children tend to reveal a higher level of social isolation, separation from the nuclear family, maternal childhood history of corporal punishment, and stressful living conditions (Daniel, Hampton, & Newberger, 1985).

Wyatt (1985) examined the prevalence of child sexual abuse through self-reports of both white and African American women. Both groups recalled the abuse occurring from 2 years to 17 years of age, but African Americans were more likely to have been abused by exposure (51%), kissing (3%), fondling (40%), rubbing of genitals (6%), and attempted intercourse (11%) than their white counterparts.

African Americans and the poor are overrepresented in child abuse and neglect statistics, and abuse among these two groups are generally judged as being more serious and more likely to be defined as abuse which requires reporting to official agencies (Zellman, 1992). Gelles and Cornell (1990) state that approximatley one in three cases of child abuse and neglect are reported to social welfare agencies. The statistics in this section were used for illustrative purposes only in an effort to underscore the pervasiveness of the problem of child abuse among African Americans. Federal, state, and local governments have formulated laws and policies in an effort not only to identify and treat these children but also to provide guidelines to aid in prevention. To ensure the implementation of these laws, policies, and guidelines, it is imperative that adequate funding be allocated to organizations that provide direct care to abused children and their families.

CHILDREARING/DISCIPLINARY PATTERNS

"I bought you into this world . . . and I will take you out!" This line from one of the earliest Cosby shows sounded unnervingly familiar to many in the show's large audience. In this particular segment, the television mom, Claire Huxtable, sounded like many African American mothers who use this familiar line in response to the antics of their children. While it is difficult to determine what " . . . I will take you out" means, this author interprets the line as meaning something very detrimental and physical. The line becomes more complex when coupled with such nonverbal behavior as frowns and a raised hand. Just as the Huxtable children knew that they should cease their mischievous behavior at the very sound of that notorious line, many African American children also understand the nature of the statement. Oral history has always been a means of passing on the legacy in the African American community and this line has been passed through generations.

Lassiter (1987) differentiates between child abuse and child abusing discipline on the basis of intent. Child abuse is viewed as intentional maltreatment whereas child abusing discipline is a maltreatment resulting from disciplinary patterns. Child abusing discipline in the African American community is transmitted intergenerationally and has been traced back to the slave experience when families modeled their discipline after that of the white slave owner. A milder form of the harsh and violent discipline levelled against the slaves developed as a survival strategy for African American families to teach their children how to avoid more violent punishment by the slave owners and to be compliant slaves (Lassiter, 1987).

The historically transmitted stress of slavery, living in a racist society, poverty, and a lack of opportunities have been associated with child abusing parents. Hampton (1987), for example, reported that caretaker stress was associated strongly with physical abuse in general, especially in nonwhite families. Poor childrearing and homemaking skills were cited in 17 percent of the families studied.

Parents of African American child victims of abuse were likely to have experienced corporal punishment as children themselves. They report being struck and spanked frequently on parts of their bodies other than their hands and bottoms (Daniel, Hampton, & Newberger, 1985). Many children are reared in homes where their parents use physical violence to solve both spousal conflicts and child disciplinary concerns (Prothrow-Stith & Spivak, 1992). Unfortunately, children raised in such violent homes were found to be at higher risk for violence in later years.

THEORETICAL MODEL AND ANALYSIS OF IMPLEMENTATION PARAMETERS

As a result of this analysis of the magnitude of the problem of child abuse and neglect and its attending legislative history, it would seem imperative that a system be implemented in which prevention—to stop the continuing cycle of violence in African American communities—is given priority. Efforts of preventive programs should ideally be focused on preventing the initial maltreatment of African American children. To do so, it is absolutely necessary to understand the causes of abuse and neglect, the multiple contexts in which they occur, and initiate programs aimed at resolving the causitive factors themselves. The complexity of the phenomenon is clear. Still, there is thought to be a relationship between the incidence of abuse and neglect and poverty-related stress within a family system (U.S. Congress, 1987; McCurdy & Daro, 1994). Inherent in that relationship is the importation of use of social services other than those dedicated specifically to child protection. Review, refinement, and implementation, of course, go hand in hand here.

If prevention cannot be effected prior to the beginning of violence, then a means must be devised to prevent reoccurrences of the abuse toward affected children. In this section, therefore, I will present a theoretical model related to the establishment and implementation of a multidisciplinary team approach in the African American community.

Figure 1 is a schematic representation of the author's interpretation of the present system as practiced in the United States. The judicial system initiates the process through the enactment of

Figure 1

Schematic Representation of Present Relationships
of Child Abuse and Neglect Professionals

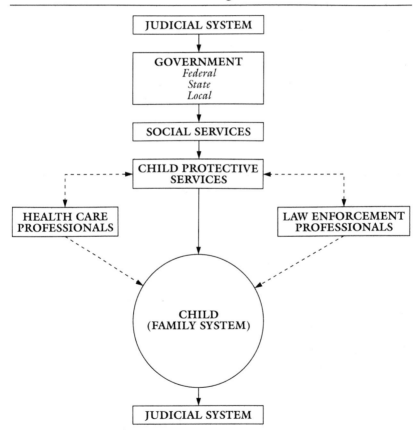

sometimes vague and ambiguous laws from which policies and guidelines are formed. Social services employees must carry out these laws and struggle with interpretations for implementation within the limited resources allocated to perform their tasks.

In many states, Child Protective Services is the agency through which all activities are coordinated, especially those of health care and law enforcement professionals who act as advisory councils to social services. In either a direct or indirect manner, these individuals impact upon the child being serviced in the system. The child may have entered the system through the mandatory reporting of one of the professionals with whom he or she came into contact. After entering the child into the social service system, the judicial system again has a part to play: deciding the disposition of a case that has already been determined by a child protective services worker as being founded; a case that must be obvious enough for the legal system to involve itself with; a case similar to that of "Little Mary Ellen."

A proposed change in the system is presented in Figure 2. This change would involve the judicial system interacting with other services throughout the process. In this way, laws, policies, and guidelines can be interpreted and refined as necessary to ensure fair and unbiased treatment. In addition, the judicial system would no longer merely provide the policies and enact them, but also aid others in their work. Through this process it is expected that the judicial system and government agencies will recognize the value of and ensure funding for continuing and expansive prevention strategies—prevention strategies which aid in breaking the cycle of violence and ensure that some cases of abuse and neglect will never occur and that others will not recur.

The model also proposes the creation of several satellite multidisciplinary teams which will be community-based and located in hospitals, schools, churches, law enforcement agencies, and within the court systems where child advocates can act as consultants. In this model, it is also vital that the African American community

Figure 2
Schematic Presentation of Proposed System of Child Abuse and
Neglect Services

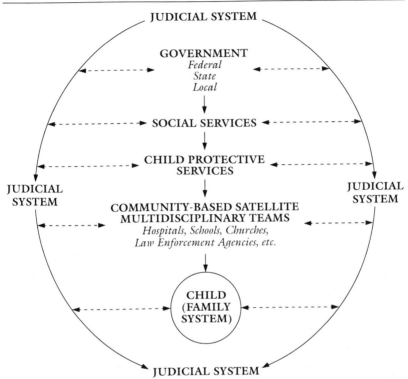

be served by persons involved on the teams who are sensitive to the
needs of the African American community and who provide culturally specific information. Nurses are in an excellent position to
handle sevsitive issues facing African Americans. Indeed, nurse educators have made multicultural issues and caring for diverse populations a staple of both undergraduate and graduate curricula.

RECOMMENDATIONS

There are no simple solutions to the issue of child abuse in the African American community because the crime is not a simple one. It is cloaked in secrecy, vague legal jargon, sketchy statistical data, and limited resources. As a result, any recommendations for solutions of the problem must be community generated and multi-faceted with far-reaching implications. Recommended strategies related to preventing child abuse are outlined in Table 2. The list is not given to imply that it is all inclusive, but rather to provide a starting point for the implementation of an organized and systematic means of preventing child abuse.

Of the proposed strategies in Table 2, the utilization of satellite multidisciplinary teams within the African American community seems most appropriate. Because of the drastic rise in child abuse, it would be a mistake to wait, solely via petition to the political forces surrounding funding, to take action. Therefore, these community-based teams should be a voluntary effort, at least initially. The teams should also be well-represented by both professionals and lay persons who have a genuine interest in the welfare of future generations. Teams can be set up in hospitals, schools, churches, law enforcement agencies, and within the court systems. Churches should be a critical entity to note as part of the team. While it is not within the scope of this chapter to discuss the role of the church in the lives of African Americans, it is necessary to underscore that involvement of the church is crucial in many African American communities. It also is of great importance that other support from the African American community is demonstrated at all levels to ensure that the treatment measure is not just one of punishment for the abusing parents and separation of the family, but is nonbiased and with a goal of family reunification. In addition, there is a need to put into place evaluation criteria to determine the effectiveness of the multidisciplinary team approaches (Hochstadt & Harwicke, 1985).

Satellite multidisciplinary teams would have several agendas to carry out: (1) developing and implementing educational programs for parents, children, and the community; (2) educating professionals who come into frequent contact with children on the cultural aspects related to discipline and child rearing practices in the African American community; (3) defining the treatment role of the teams; and (4) developing consistent functions that can be replicated by other agencies. Each of these teams would be interdependent with the local department of social services' child protection division. In this way, the team's activities would be coordinated to make maximum use of resources. Additionally, the child protective services workers would have access to a myriad of community individuals who are knowledgeable and genuinely interested in the prevention of child abuse.

It is envisioned that these satellite multidisciplinary teams would function as code blue teams and operate in acute care hospitals; that is, each high risk child would be treated with the same vigor and energy as cardiac arrest patients. As the goal of a code blue team is to prevent the death of the patient, the goal of the satellite multidisciplinary team would be to prevent an occurrence or a reoccurrence of child abuse. The team would respond initially to the needs of the child by assessing the situation in terms of abuse and neglect. This assessment would require obtaining both subjective and objective data from the child, parents, teachers, relatives, ministers, and others qualified to note the child's experiences.

With this available data, the team would then proceed to make its analysis of the particular situation. The data analysis would also provide a more extensive basis for the planning, implementation, and evaluation of strategies needed to prevent abuse and neglect community wide. The strategies implemented should not only reflect the expertise of the team members, but should also be culturally specific and reflect the resources of any referral agencies. Within this context, nurses can act as resource persons who have expertise in handling issues of a sensitive nature. Furthermore, every

Table 2

Recommended Strategies Related to Child Abuse/Neglect Prevention

Strategy	Purpose	Actors Involved
I. Satellite Multidisciplinary Teams Voluntary and Community-Based • Hospitals • Schools • Law Enforcement Agencies • Court System	• To develop and implement culturally sensitive educational programs for parents and children • To educate professionals who come into frequent contact with children • To develop consistent functions • To define the role of the teams	Social services workers, community leaders, ministers, health care professionals, educators, law enforcement professionals, parents, and legislators
II. Conferences • National • Local	• To discuss, review, refine present laws • To develop congruency between state laws • To brainstorm on other strategies • To provide public forums	Legislators, social workers, health care professionals, educators, law enforcement professionals, parents, who can contribute to the expansion of knowledge on child abuse and neglect
III. Evaluation of Present Programs	• To develop summative and formative evaluation criteria • To develop strategies for the implementation of evaluation programs	State and local Departments of Social Services, Multidisciplinary teams, Churches, Community Volunteers

| IV. | Allocation of Resources | • To evaluate utilization of funds being allocated to various programs and redirect those funds as needed for support of effective programs
• To increase appropriations for research aimed at the prevention of both initial occurrences and reoccurrences | U.S. Department of Health and Human Services, legislators, child advocate lobbying groups |
| V. | Research and Development | • To refine programs which are found to be effective
• To provide information to governing bodies, social service agencies, and the general public
• To determine causes and risk factors that respond to treatment
• To develop a profile of the abuser | U.S. Department of Health and Human Services, National Center on Child Abuse and Neglect, professionals in health, law enforcement, social services, education |

effort should be made to involve the child and the parents in the establishment of the treatment goals. An individual evaluation of each intervention would need to be made to determine: (1) a prognosis for the child (family); (2) any common risk factors; (3) the effectiveness of treatment programs; and (4) strategies that will improve the functioning of the teams.

CONCLUSION

In this chapter, I have presented an overview of the problem of child abuse and neglect among African Americans as a multiphasic community health care issue in need of improved prevention, identification, and treatment programs. The statistical data available provides only a global picture of the issue. Further analysis is needed to determine, more specifically, what trends, if any, exist in the African American community. The statistical analysis did reveal that the number of African American children abused and/or neglected is rising and that African Americans continue to be over represented. I urge that further research be conducted in the area of discipline and child rearing practices within and among various ethnic groups with special attention to the variances in the African American community.

The recommendations proposed here, and with an emphasis on the development of satellite multidisciplinary teams to be set up in churches, hospitals, schools, law enforcement agencies, and court systems, have the potential of establishing an interdisciplinary structure at least cognizant of the complexity of the issue. These teams would aid in furthering the awareness of child abuse and neglect issues among professional and lay persons. Prevention of abuse and neglect would be aided mainly through the educational and evaluative team functions via culturally sensitive and specific information.

REFERENCES

Child Abuse Prevention and Treatment Act of 1974, §1191, 42 U.S.C. §5101.

Daniel, J. H., Hampton, R. L., & Newberger, E. H. (1987). Child abuse and accidents in black families: A controlled comparative study. In R. L. Hampton, (Ed.), *Violence in the black family* (pp. 55–65). Lexington: Heath.

Gelles, R. J., & Cornell, C. P. (1990). *Intimate violence in families.* (2nd ed.). Newbury Park, CA: Sage Publications.

Hampton, R. L. (1987). Violence against black children: Current knowledge and future research needs. In R. L. Hampton, (Ed.), *Violence in the black family* (pp. 1–20). Lexington: Heath.

Hochstadt, N. J., & Harwicke, N. J. (1985). How effective is the multidisciplinary approach? A follow-up study. *Child Abuse & Neglect, 9,* 365–367.

Kempe, C. H., Silverman, F. N., Steele, B. F., Droegemueller, W., & Silver, H. K. (1962). The battered child syndrome. *Journal of the American Medical Association, 181,* 107–112.

Lassiter, R. F. (1987). Child rearing in black families: Child abusing discipline. In R. L. Hampton, (Ed.), *Violence in the black family* (pp. 39–53). Lexington: Heath.

McCurdy, K., & Daro, D. (1994). *Current trends in child abuse reporting and fatalities: The results of the 1993 annual fifty states survey.* Chicago, IL: NCPCA.

Mr. Bergh enlarging his sphere of usefulness. (1874, April). *The New York Times.*

Protection for children. (1874, December). *The New York Times.*

Prothrow-Stith, D., & Spivak, H. (1992). Homicide and violence: Contemporary health problems for America's black community. In R. L. Braithwaite, & S. E. Taylor, (Eds.), *Health issues in the black community* (pp. 132–143). San Francisco: Jossey-Bass Publishers.

Sloan, I. J. (Ed.). (1983). *Child abuse: Governing law and legislation.* London: Oceana.

U.S. Bureau of the Census. (1993). *Statistical abstract of the United States: 1993* (113th edition) Washington, D.C.

U.S. Congress, House of Representatives, Select Committee on Children, Youth, and Families. (1987). Abused children in America: Victims of official neglect (House Report, pp. 100–260). Washington, DC: U.S. Government Printing Office.

Wyatt, G. E. (1985). The sexual abuse of Afro-Americans and White-American women in childhood. *Child Abuse & Neglect, 9,* 507–519.

Zellman, G. L. (1992). The impact of case characteristics on child abuse reporting decisions. *Child Abuse & Neglect, 16,* 57–74.

Chapter Four

African American Children, Adolescents, and Chronic Illness

DeLois P. Weekes

The database concerning chronic illness among African American children and adolescents is uneven. There are no existing statistics which present a national picture of the prevalence of chronic illness in black children and adolescents. Existing demographic and epidemiological information about this subpopulation is fragmented, contradictory, or limited to geographical regions served by a specific program (Sterling, 1992). Therefore, of necessity, this chapter draws from studies and theoretical discussions of nonblack children and adolescents to provide us with information about how black children, adolescents, and their families may be affected by chronic illness.

It is estimated that 10 to 15 percent (more than 7.5 million) of all children and adolescents experience a chronic illness between birth and 18 years of age (Hobbs, Perrin, & Ireys, 1985; Rose & Thomas, 1989). Due to technological advances in pharmacology, surgery, and medicine, chronically ill children and adolescents are surviving and living longer (Newacheck & Taylor, 1992). In fact, there has been a two- to seven-fold increase in the survival rates for children and adolescents with illnesses such as diabetes, sickle cell disease, and pediatric cancer. consequently, attention is focused on how these young people cope with day-to-day realities and demands of growing up chronically ill (Weekes & Savedra, 1988).

ANALYTIC FRAMEWORK

This chapter focuses on the impact of chronic illness on black children, adolescents, and their families. Figure 1 presents an analytic model of how chronic illness affects black children and adolescents. This model functions as a framework for examining and organizing the information presented here. In this chapter, I hope to demonstrate that a broad array of factors in interaction function to determine outcomes for black children and adolescents who are growing up chronically ill. The model, which is also representative of a life-span developmental perspective as derived from developmental psychology, describes the impact of historical, concurrent, normative and non-normative variables on developmental change as it occurs within the context of life circumstances and experiences (growing up chronically ill as a black child or adolescent).

Figure 1

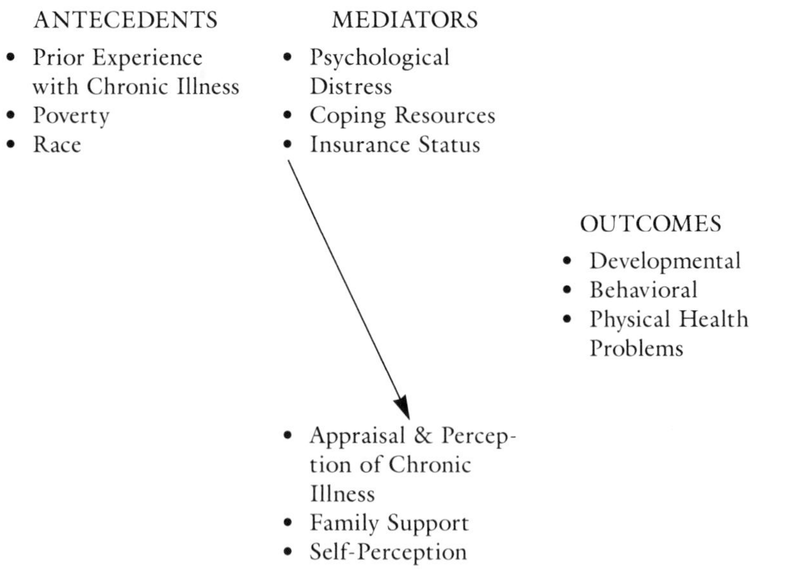

ANTECEDENTS
- Prior Experience with Chronic Illness
- Poverty
- Race

MEDIATORS
- Psychological Distress
- Coping Resources
- Insurance Status

OUTCOMES
- Developmental
- Behavioral
- Physical Health Problems

- Appraisal & Perception of Chronic Illness
- Family Support
- Self-Perception

The life span developmental perspective focuses on the community of life events that conjointly influence a person's response to particular events or experiences (Baltes, Reese, & Lipsitt, 1980). The occurrence of chronic illness in childhood or adolescence functions as historical antecedents that alter the adolescent's or young adult's view of self, as well as his or her relationships with family and peers, society, and the world. From a life span perspective, developmental change is influenced by three primary antecedent influences: normative age-graded, normative history-graded, and non-normative factors (Baltes, Reese, & Lipsitt, 1980). Normative age-graded factors are defined as person-related biological and developmental determinents that are correlated with chronological age; for example, menarche and entering school (Weekes, 1991). Normative history-graded influences are defined as general events or event patterns, such as any form of slavery or racism experienced by a particular group (Weekes, 1991). Black children living in the twentieth century, and in the United States, have not experienced literal enslavement. Nonetheless, they may have encountered racist attitudes and behaviors (associated with race, culture, or socioeconomic status). Such encounters may engender self-perceptions that are akin to those born of actual enslavement, and these self-perceptions can impact behavior and responses to present experiences. Typically, history-graded events affect particular cohorts (black children and adolescents growing up during the same time periods) in varied ways and thus serve as important determinants of developmental change. Non-normative influences are defined as environmental and biological determinants; that is, diagnosis with a chronic illness that, while significant relative to its effect on development, is not universal in its occurrence (Weekes, 1991).

Three principal themes emerge from the life span approach: (1) developmental change occurs across the entire life span and is influenced by physical, psychological, and social factors; (2) life events and trajectories are products of a complex, cumulative interweaving of behavior and personality that has dimensions of both continuity and discontinuity; and (3) people are agents of change in their own development, and have the capacity to select, ignore, and modify life experiences.

Developmental Change

Biological Factors. Biological factors have to do with physical or pathophysiological changes engendered by chronic illness. Chronically ill children and adolescents are defined as those who have one or more chronic conditions that cause them to experience pain, discomfort, or being upset often or all of the time, for a period greater than three months duration, or that limits them in their ability to participate in important activities of daily living (playing, attending school, or being with peers) (Aday et al., 1993).

In a study of health care needs of a multiethnic group of adolescents, at least one chronic condition associated with significant morbidity or functional impairment in daily living was found in 15 percent of children and adolescents (Fitzpatrick et al., 1990). Chronic diseases included asthma 8 percent, congenital heart disease 4 percent, renal disease 1.4 percent, musculoskeletal deformity 1.2 percent, seizure disorder 0.6 percent, and sickle cell disease 0.3 percent. Chronic illnesses such as these are characterized by frequent complications, unpredictable courses, pain, physical discomfort, as well as psychological distress (Revell & Liptak, 1991). Chronic illness, we should remember, is a lifelong presence; there are usually no cures. Treatments, such as chemotherapy, bracing, injections, and respiratory therapy are often difficult and sometimes embarrassing (Revel et al., 1991). Findings from this study are fairly general to any chronically ill child. Black chronically ill children, however, may have to deal with similar problems plus substandard housing, unsafe neighborhoods where drug dealers are the norm, as well as school systems that are less than optimal. These living conditions make dealing with the constant presence of a chronic illness even more challenging. In part, this accounts for the poorer outcomes, greater frequency of relapses, increased hospitalizations, and more secondary complications in blacks than are typically seen in white chronically ill children.

Psychological Factors. Psychological factors refer to the impact of chronic illness on the achievement of developmental tasks as well as to the potential occurrence of behavioral or mental health problems. The accomplishment of developmental tasks is made more difficult by the extra demands associated with the chronic illness. Typical developmental needs—autonomy, individuation, socialization with peers, and independence—interact with the chronic illness demands, producing increased forms and varieties of stress. Taken together, prolonged stress and psychological distress increase the overall risk of behavioral as well as mental health problems (Patterson & Geber, 1991). From several epidemiologic studies, there are indications of approximately a two-fold increase in behavioral and mental health problems in children and adolescents with chronic illness (Gortmaker, Walker, Weitzman, & Sobol, 1990; National Center for Health Statistics, 1985). While these data are general to all racial groups, it is reasonable to expect that the outcomes would not be appreciably different for chronically ill black children and adolescents. However, during discussions with mothers of black chronically ill children, this author has been made acutely aware of the differential treatment they receive. For example, one mother indicated that when she dressed in jeans and a sweat shirt she was treated as though she knew nothing and was not listened to by health care providers. As a result, and even when her child was in crisis, she would take time to change clothes and put on her best outfit. Another mother, who had read widely about her child's diabetes and was quite knowledgeable, told of a white physician who berated her for her effort, saying, "a little knowledge was a dangerous thing for some people." Clearly, this kind of differential treatment alienates black parents from the health care system and contributes to their reticence to take their children for preventive follow-up care. A situation is created where health outcomes for black chronically ill children indeed may be worse than for white chronically ill children.

Social Factors. Social factors refer to environmental and family variables that impinge on developmental, behavioral, and health outcomes for black children and adolescents who are chronically ill. These factors include poverty, economic decline, and health insurance status.

During the 1980s, the proportion of black children and adolescents living in poverty soared. Specifically, from 1979 to 1985, the rate of poverty for black children/adolescents 18 years and under rose from 36 percent to 45 percent, compared to an increase from 12 percent to 13 percent for white children during the same time period (Duncan, 1988; McLoyd, 1990) Families of black children and adolescents also are more likely to experience drops in family income relative to overall need. Such economic declines are associated with increasing joblessness, and increased numbers of black female-headed households (McLoyd, 1990). Over the last decade, the number of black families headed by women has more than tripled. Currently, approximately 45 percent of black children and adolescents live in female-headed households. Of these children, 70 percent are considered to be at or below the poverty line, compared to 24 percent of black children who live in two-parent families (McLoyd, 1990). Other factors that have negative implications for black families are the outgrowth of the interaction of social, economic, and political factors. For example, when economic conditions worsen, there is usually a demand for changes in social policies, especially those relating to social programs dedicated to regional and state provisions for services to children with special health care needs. When such programs are cut or discontinued, black families with chronically ill children suffer disproportionately because they have few alternative options.

Due to their disproportionate representation among the uninsured, children are on the front lines of the health care crisis (Future of Children, 1993). Indeed, the Kids Count profile (1992) revealed that, throughout the decade of the 1980s, the nation made no progress or slipped backwards in seven to nine measures of health and child well-being. In 1992, 12.7 percent of all children had no health insurance coverage for the entire year. As a result, approximately 8.4 million children 18 years and younger had no access to mainstream health care. A recent study conducted by the USA Foundation (1993) predicts that approximately 16 million, or one-fourth of all children, will be without insurance at some point during the year. Study results also indicated that more than 80 percent of those uninsured live in families where at least one parent is employed. Without insurance, chronically ill children and adolescents do not have access to needed preventive and illness-related services. The Report of the Secretary's Task Force on Black and Minority Health (1985) also concluded that there is a serious, if general, disparity in health status between blacks and whites. The combination of health status disparity and lack of insurance potentially interact to exacerbate negative health outcomes for chronically ill black children and adolescents.

Children and adolescents live and develop within the context of families. It is important to note, therefore, that chronic illness is not only experienced by the child/adolescent, but also by the family (Patterson et al., 1990). Lewis (1990) suggests here that a chronic illness diagnosis invades the entire family, not just the diagnosed patient's body. As a result of a chronic illness diagnosis, family routines, activities, and perceptions change, as do daily life patterns, which become less predictable. In addition to maintaining an environment that is appropriate to the care and development of family members, the family must also respond and adjust to the continuous changes and demands of the chronic illness (Gonzalez & Reiss, 1983). In this effort, the family takes on a new identity, differentiates itself from other families, reorganizes, and develops new ways of operating in order to better cope with ongoing multiple demands engendered by the presence of a child or adolescent member with a chronic illness. Gonzalez and Reiss (1983) note the striking fact that very few families adequately cope with and manage both the demands of the chronic illness and the demands of the rest of family life. Rather, the family either reorganizes around the illness and the patient, or they exclude the illness to some degree and go on with life. The coping stance selected by the family will invariably affect the way in which the child or adolescent copes with the illness and his or her relationship to the family.

Promotion of positive developmental outcomes in chronically ill black children and adolescents may be potentiated by activation of protective factors or capabilities to manage the increased demands and stress. Achieving a balance between the illness-related tasks and protective variables that aid in the management of these demands can be helpful here (Albee, 1982). Protective variables include: (1) intrapersonal factors such as a sense of self-efficacy (ability to enact behaviors that bring about desired outcomes), coping resources, as well as perception and appraisal of the illness as not only a challenge but also an opportunity; (2) family and extended family supports; and (3) environmental factors such as access to health care.

CONTINUITY AND DISCONTINUITY IN RESPONSE TO CHRONIC ILLNESS

The life span orientation also addresses the issues of continuity and discontinuity relative to responses to chronic illness. Inherent in the notion of continuity is the presumption of predictability of patterns of behavior change during childhood and adolescence (Baltes, Cornelius, & Nesselroade, 1979). Such predictability is based on a delineation of explanatory principles that are presumed to be relevant across childhood and adolescence. In addition, these explanatory principles have typically emerged from a number of theoretical perspectives which share a common listing of developmental tasks that children and adolescents achieve as they progress toward adulthood. Often, these developmental tasks are viewed as explanatory and predictive of behavioral change across childhood, and early, middle, and late adolescence. For example, by using Erikson's (1963) fourth stage of psychological development (industry versus shame and doubt) as an explanatory principle, a researcher would predict that the school-age child who successfully achieved industry would also achieve successful identity as an adolescent. However, such predictions often miss the mark. Erikson would explain such common inaccuracy of prediction on the basis of unsuccessful achievement of industry. The life span developmentalist would counter by saying that each prior developmental stage is preparatory only to a degree, and is therefore not relevant across the adolescent life course (Weekes, 1991). The argument is clarifying. Because eventual discontinuity will occur, developmental tasks and stages are at best imperfect explanatory principles. Indeed, when applied to black children and adolescents, these developmental tasks may have even less explanatory, predictive usefulness than when applied, for example, to white children and adolescents.

Focus on continuity without recognition of concomitant discontinuity, and inherent racial/ethnic bias may lead researchers and health care professionals to accept the notion that once one identifies the developmental tasks facing black children and adolescents, and where a particular child or adolescent fits into the various stages, it will be fairly easy to predict developmental change in behavior. In reality, however, children and adolescents are not all alike. They differ widely, even relative to the normative age-graded influences on development. Because it is not possible to predict the exact point at which a particular chronically ill child or adolescent will enter or exit puberty, ranges are helpful. Each individual brings to an experience a history of attitudes, situational responses, and racial and family backgrounds. This history has strong influence on individual response to each of the developmental tasks any child or adolescent faces.

Black Children and Adolescents as Agents of Change

A person's ability to act to alter or change his or her view of a situation constitutes one aspect of resilience; that is, reframing an experience or mobilizing resources as a means of dealing with adverse circumstances. This type of resilience may be manifest through individual coping behavior or development of broader family and extended family supports.

Coping Behavior. Diagnosis with chronic illnesses such as cancer, diabetes, or asthma involves attendant stressors like repeated hospitalizations, procedural and diagnostic treatments, illness-related therapy, episodic separation from peers and family, and alterations in physical appearance. Coping is the means by which the children and adolescents who are growing up chronically ill deal with the competing demands made by the chronic illness and the attending biological, psychosocial, and emotional changes. Coping consists of cognitive and behavioral efforts to master, tolerate, reduce, or minimize environmental and internal demands and conflicts (Lazarus & Folkman, 1985). Van Dongen-Melman and colleagues (1986) have proposed a model that addresses the potential stressors of chronic illness. Based on this model, stressors are those events that are perceived by the adolescent to cause changes in self-perception (perceived specialness and perceived vulnerability) as well as uncertainty. These perceived stressors can occur concurrently and can vary in intensity. Their individual or conjoint effects precipitate a need for coping on the part of chronically ill adolescents.

Changes in Self-Perception. Children and adolescents vary in their resilience and response to chronic illness. Perception of self as particularly special or vulnerable is a seminal psychosocial response.

Perceived Specialness. Perceived specialness is characterized by hopefulness as well as trust and reliance on a Greater Being to provide care and protection. To illustrate, Hinds and Martin (1988, p. 338) cite the example of a 12-year-old girl with cancer who stated, "I just tell myself that God will decide what is best for my life and no matter if he decides if I live or die, he'll decide the right thing." As a result, the need to be anxious or to be overly concerned about possible health outcomes was, at least for her, ameliorated. In addition, adolescents with cancer often express the belief that the Greater Being may have selected them especially to be afflicted as a means of improving their character (Weekes, 1989).

This sense of "being singled out" was illustrated by adolescents who reported believing themselves to be stronger and more capable as a result of having cancer, of having a closer relationship with "God," and of being selected by "God" to get the disease because "He" wanted to make them better people (Kellerman, Ellenberg, Dash, & Rigler, 1980). For example, a 15-year-old girl stated, "Before I got cancer I was hanging out a lot and drinking and doing drugs. Since I got cancer, I feel closer to God, I pray more, eat better, and I'm not doing alcohol and drugs no more." Viewing the diagnosis of a chronic illness as a positive factor that contributes to improvements in self is a form of secondary appraisal that facilitates coping. The perception of self as special is associated with attribution of positive outcomes to the chronic illness diagnosis and its related treatment. Such positive attribution enables the adolescent to be hopeful and to believe that over time he or she will learn more about the treatments, get used to them, know what to expect, and be able to alter and improve a difficult situation (Kellern et al., 1980; Weekes, 1989).

Perceived Vulnerability. Perceived vulnerability is related to the degree to which adolescents believe themselves to have oversight and self-mastery over the chronic illness and its treatment. Children and adolescents diagnosed with asthma and diabetes have been found to perceive themselves to have more individual control, and reported less perceived vulnerability than adolescents diagnosed with illnesses over which there was little perceived control (e.g., cancer, renal disease, and heart disease) (Kellerman et al., 1980). Children and adolescents with cancer, renal, and cardiac disease reported perceiving themselves to be at the mercy of the physician and the medical system for control of their illness, and they perceived their individual control and competence were severely decreased. This perception is illustrated by the response of a 16-year-old white male who stated, "The disease controls my body, the doctors control the disease and they both rule my life. Then my parents treat me like a baby and won't let me do anything other kids do" (Weekes, 1989).

Perceived vulnerability is inextricably bound to the child's and the adolescent's appraisal of the chronic illness and its treatment as taxing or exceeding his or her opportunity to exercise personal control and mastery. From infancy onward, one of the major developmental thrusts is the achievement of ever increasing control of the self and the immediate environment (Blum, 1984). Certain chronic illnesses and their related treatment threaten the normal trajectory of the adolescent's development. The unpredictability associated with these chronic illnesses induces considerable uncertainty regarding attainment of developmental markers such as autonomy and independence. Clearly, the struggle between dependence and independence is greatly exacerbated by the demands for reliance on the skills and support of parents, medical and nursing staff, and the medical care system for some adolescents growing up chronically ill. Lability of illness and fluctuation between acute and chronic periods creates imbalance in the adolescent's life and requires constant redefinition of the self-identity (whether to view self as an ill or not ill person). It also necessitates constant change in expected performance ability on the part of both the adolescent and parents.

Family Supports. The presence of competing demands and stresses from both chronic illness and daily life tasks stimulates families to develop or expand family and extended family supports and networks. This is particularly true for black families who have chronically ill children and adolescents. In this regard, one mother told this author that when her child was sick, she called on god parents, her play mother, spiritual parents, and anyone else she thought might be able to help her (she never let pride get in her way). Relatives and non-relatives (by mainstream definition) or temporary relatives frequently comprise the primary closely knit group.

For the most part, the family may be constant, with changes occurring consistently through life events such as the diagnosis of a chronic illness in a child or adolescent member. Distant kin or non-kin who are nevertheless considered to be family members may be more or less a part of the extended family network, and they may play greater or lesser parts in the family as needs and demands dictate. The extended family may be a parent's most important support network, and members may be expected to contribute information, make personal sacrifices, or contribute in other ways for the sake of the family. Black families with children or adolescents diagnosed with a chronic illness respond in whatever ways and by whatever means necessary to ensure that they have what they need to continue as a family and to cope with the illness.

In summary, the life span orientation provides a guiding perspective that may be used to determine the historical and contemporary influences on black child/adolescence development as they occur within a chronic illness context. Here, how black children and adolescents respond to growing up chronically ill is viewed as a function of historical (past) and current life experiences. Of specific importance is the context of psychological distress. How the black child or adolescent deals with psychological distress during childhood will in part determine how he or she deals with it in later life. A cautionary note here, however, is in order: Use of a theoretical perspective should never cause a researcher to lose sight of the ubiquitous social, economic, and political conditions that contribute to the disproportional treatment of black children in U.S. society. Furthermore, the guiding theoretical and conceptual framework must be filtered through the contextual conditions of racism and bigotry that continue to mitigate against the health of black children and adolescents.

REFERENCES

Aday, L. A., Lee, E. S., Spears, B., Chung, C. W., Youssef, A., & Bloom, B. (1993). Health insurance and utilization of medical care for children with special health care needs. *Medical Care, 31*(11), 1013–1026.

Alby, N. (1982). Ending the chemotherapy of acute leukemia: A period of difficult weaning. In J. L. Schulman, & J. Kupst (Eds.), *The child with cancer* (pp. 175–182). Springfield, IL: Charles C. Thomas.

Anderson, P. P., & Fenichel, E. S. (1989). Serving culturally diverse families of infants and toddlers with disabilities. National Center for Clinical Infant Programs.

Baltes, P. B., Reese, H. W., & Lipsitt, L. P. (1980). Life-span developmental psychology. *Annual Review of Psychology, 31,* 63–110.

Baltes, P. B., Cornelius, S. W., & Nesselroade, J. R. (1979). Cohort effects in developmental psychology. In J. R. Nesselroade, & P. B. Baltes (Eds.), *Longitudinal research in the study of behavior and development.* San Diego, CA: Academic Press.

Blum, R. W. (1984). *Chronic illness and disabilities in childhood and adolescence.* San Francisco: Grune & Stratton.

Duncan, G. (1988). The economic environment of childhood. Paper presented at a study group meeting on poverty and children, University of Kansas, Lawrence.

Erikson, E. (1963). *Childhood and society* (2nd rev. ed.). New York: Norton.

Featherman, D. (1983). Life-span perspectives in social science research. In P. B. Baltes & O. G. Brim (Eds.), *Life-span development and behavior* (pp. 1–57). San Diego, CA: Academic Press.

Families USA Foundation. (1993). Half of us: Families priced out of health protection. Washington, DC: Families USA Foundation.

Fitzpatrick, S. B., Fujii, C., Shragg, L. R., Morgan, M., & Felice, A. M. (1990). Do health care needs of indigent Mexican-American, Black, and White adolescents differ? *Journal of Adolescent Health Care, 11,* 128–132.

Gonzalez, S., & Reiss, D. (1983). The family and chronic illness: Technical difficulties in assessing adjustment. Unpublished manuscript.

Gortmaker, S. L., Walker, D. K., Weitzman, M., & Sobol, A. M. (1990). Chronic conditions, socioeconomic risks, and behavioral problems in children and adolescents. *Pediatrics, 85*(3), 267–276.

Hanson, C. L., Henggler, S. W., & Burghen, G. A. (1987). Race and sex difference in metabolic control of adolescents with IDDM: A function of psychological variables? *Diabetes Care, 10*(3), 313–318.

Hinds, P., & Martin, J. (1988). Hopefulness and the self-sustaining process in adolescents with cancer. *Nursing Research, 37*, 336–340.

Hobbs, N., Perrin, & Ireys, H. (1985). *Chronically ill children and their families.* San Francisco: Jossey-Bass.

Kellerman, J., Zeltzer, L., Ellenberg, L., Dash, J., & Rigler, D. (1980). Psychological effects of illness in adolescence: Anxiety, self-esteem, and perception of control. *Journal of Pediatrics, 97*(1), 126–131.

Kids Count Data Book. (1992). State profiles of child well-being. The Annie E. Casey Foundation.

Lazarus, R., & Folkman, S. (1985). *Stress, appraisal and coping.* New York.

Lewis, F. M. (1990). Strengthening family supports, cancer and the family. *Cancer, 65*(3), 752–759.

McAdoo, H. (1986, May). Black kinship. *Psychology Today,* 67–110.

McLoyd, V. (1990). The impact of economic hardship on black families and children: Psychological distress, parenting, and socioeconomic development. *Child Development, 61,* 311–346.

National Center for Health Statistics (1985). Summary of data on handicapped children and youth. Cambridge, MA: Human Services Research Institute.

National Institute of Nursing Research. (1993). Health promotion for older children and adolescents. U.S. Department of Health and Human Services. U.S. Public Health Service, National Institutes of Health.

Newacheck, J., & Taylor, W. R. (1992). Childhood chronic illness: Prevalence, severity, and impact. *American Journal of Public Health, 82*(3), 364–437.

Patterson, J. M., & Gerber, G. (1991). Preventing mental health problems in children with chronic illness or disability. *Child Health Chronicle, 20*(3), 150–161.

Revell, G. M., & Liptak, G. S. (1991). Understanding the child with special health care needs: A developmental perspective. *Journal of Pediatric Nursing, 6*(4), 258–268.

Rose, J. H., & Thomas, R. B. (1989). *Children with chronic conditions.* Orlando: Grune & Stratton.

Sterling, Y. (1992). African American Families who have chronically ill children. Presented as part of the Proceedings of the 6th Annual Black Nurses Symposium. School of Nursing, University of California, San Francisco.

Sterling, Y., Peterson, J., & Weekes, D. P. (in review). African American families with chronically ill children: A critical review of the literature.

The Future of Children. (1993). Center for the future of children: The David and Lucille Packard Foundation.

Van Dongen-Melman, J. E. W. M., Pruyn, J. F. A., Van Zanen, G. E., & Sanders-Woudstra, J. A. R. (1986). Coping with childhood cancer: A conceptual view. *Journal of Psychococial Oncology, 4*($^1/_2$), 147–161.

Weekes, D. P., & Savedra, M. (1988). Adolescent cancer: Coping with treatment-related pain. *Journal of Pediatric Nursing, 3*(5), 318–327.

Weekes, D. P. (1989). Adolescents with cancer: Correlates of intra-individual change in type of coping strategy. Doctoral dissertation. University of CA, San Francisco.

Weekes, D. P. (1991). Application of the life-span developmental perspective to nursing research with adolescents. *Journal of Pediatric Nursing, 6*(1), 38–48.

Chapter Five

Norfolk State University Resource Mothers Program: A Community Response to Adolescent Pregnancy

Agnes M. Richardson-Collins and
Antoinette A. Coleman

Angela is a 14-year-old African American, middle school student. She is five months pregnant and has no access to prenatal care. She resides with her stepfather, mother, and three sisters in Norfolk, Virginia. Angela is the third oldest child in the family. They live in a low-income urban area. Angela has managed to conceal her pregnancy from her mother and stepfather. She is an average student. Angela became ill in school and was required to report to the school health clinic. The school nurse asked Angela if she was receiving prenatal care and her response was quick and direct: "No, I'll just go to the Community Hospital when it's time."

While this vignette may seem dramatic, unfortunately it represents the behavior of many teenagers, especially African American teens, who become pregnant. Even with the tremendous progress in our health care system over the past decades to advance medical practices, educate consumers on good health care practices, and increase health care providers, African American teens remain a major at-risk population among adolescents who become pregnant (Edelman, 1987).

It is estimated that over one million teenage girls become pregnant annually in the United States. Of this population, more than 30,000 of these pregnant adolescents fall under the age of 15, with African Americans representing a large proportion of the population

(Stanhope & Lancaster, 1992). In 1992, there were 936 births to teenagers in Norfolk, Virginia. Of these 936 births, 593 were to African Americans, 326 were to whites, and 17 were to other races (State of Virginia, 1992).

The number of teens who become pregnant is undoubtedly astounding. However, it is not just "the number of girls who become pregnant" that makes adolescent pregnancy a crisis challenging many social, and socially dedicated, institutions (i.e., health care, families, schools). Bernstein (1982) identified teenage pregnancy as an extension of an emotional and social crisis compounded by the developmental task of adolescents. The results of this crisis are increased psychological and physiological stressors for the adolescent and society.

In Norfolk, Virginia, health care providers, schools, and social welfare agencies are faced with increasing numbers of adolescent pregnancies each year. In addition to the number of girls becoming pregnant, these systems are confronted with the problems associated with teens attempting to cope with (1) pregnancy, (2) parenting, (3) personal issues, and (4) socioeconomic dilemmas.

The aforementioned problems associated with adolescent pregnancy result in the number of teens who do not access prenatal care early during their pregnancy, maintain well-baby check-ups, develop good birth control practices, and complete their education after the birth of their baby. In many cases, these conditions have long-term negative effects on the mother and baby. More than any other group, African Americans represent a higher proportion of pregnant teens experiencing these conditions during and after their pregnancies (Edelman, 1987).

First, teens are a generally high-risk population for not accessing early prenatal care. Teens who do not get prenatal care early increase their chances of low birth weight births and infant mortality among babies born to them. The United States, we must remember, does not fare well among developed nations for decreasing infant mortality, ranking an embarrasing twentieth (Stanhope &

Lancaster, 1992). Furthermore, the risk of infant mortality, low birth weight births, and complications associated with pregnancy are experienced by teenagers more often than by their older counterparts. Thus, for teens who do not receive early prenatal care, childbearing can become a high-risk situation for both mother and baby.

In 1992, there were 119 low birth weight births in the city of Norfolk, Virginia. Eighty-eight births were to African Americans, 30 were to whites, and 1 was to other race. The infant mortality rate for the city was 17.9 per 1,000 live births, in comparison to 9.0 per 1,000 live births nationally (State of Virginia, 1992).

In terms of total numbers, there were 97 deaths reported for infants born to teen mothers in Norfolk, Virginia, in 1992. Of these reported infant deaths, 62 were to African Americans, 33 were to whites, and 2 were to other races. When comparing Norfolk to other health districts in the Commonwealth of Virginia, the higher infant death rate is quite clear (State of Virginia, 1992).

The need to develop ongoing intervention strategies for pregnant teens to access prenatal care, especially during the first trimester of pregnancy, cannot be overemphasized. Empirical data indicate there is a lower incidence of infant mortality, low birth weight births, and morbidity for women who access prenatal care during the first trimester of pregnancy (Garzon & Benjamin-Coleman, 1993).

In contemporary U.S. society, it is quite often implied and assumed that every woman who becomes pregnant will access prenatal care early in her pregnancy. This perception cannot be further from the truth, particularly where teens are concerned and especially African American teens. As a whole, pregnant teens represent the largest percentage of pregnant women who do not receive prenatal care during the first trimester of their pregnancy (Sarafino, 1990), and the large number of African American teens in this group is more than telling.

ACCESS: REALITIES AND CONSEQUENCES

Numerous efforts have been made at the federal, state, and local levels to increase the number of teens who access prenatal care, particularly those teens cited as most vulnerable and difficult to reach—African Americans and Hispanics. Many of these efforts are incremental approaches, based on overreaching fiscal policies, that focus primarily on defraying the cost of health care services (i.e., Medicaid) for the teen mother. Access is another matter altogether. Giving a pregnant teen a Medicaid card, for example, does not mean she will access the prenatal care available to her.

To further illustrate this problem, let us turn, again, to Medicaid itself. Medicaid focuses primarily on the concrete issue of reducing the burden of health care cost to the recipient. Medicaid does not address the complex psychosocial needs of pregnant and parenting teens, which often become overwhelming. We know all too well the intense emotional support pregnant and parenting teens need to cope effectively with their physiological treatment during pregnancy and the birth of their baby. Simple access to public assisstance which covers only *medical* expenditures is just not enough. Add to this the kinds of incremental social programs that are available in conjunction with Medicaid, compounded by recent nationwide and state cutbacks in total expenditures for such programs, and the problem grows ever more complex.

Access is not sustained at optimal levels nor is access itself sufficient to deal adequately with the human problems that exist.

At the very least, this population of teens require ongoing supportive programs that operate from a holistic model designed to pull services together *for them*. As further research will indicate, for many reasons, it is simply too common for teens not to access the prenatal health care they need early on during their pregnancy even when Medicaid is available.

Although educational programs have been designed to stress the importance of accessing prenatal care early, they have often failed to address the socioenvironmental barriers (i.e., developmental stage of mother, stability of living environment, cultural beliefs, support systems, education, socioeconomic status, acceptance of pregnancy) that impede the use of health care services by African American and Hispanic teen mothers. Because many of these programs are void of addressing issues of cultural diversity, and like Medicaid operate within a fragmented services delivery system, pregnant or parenting teens do not wish to use or do not have sufficient knowledge to access such programs.

Garzon and Benjamin-Coleman (1993) cite that women who delay accessing prenatal care until the second and third trimester associated their behavior with (1) denying pregnancy, (2) lack of family support, (3) the attitudes exhibited by health care providers, (4) excessive time spent waiting to receive services, (5) the provision of inadequate health care services, and (6) lack of available transportation services. Denying pregnancy and family support were the least important issues impacting those not accessing prenatal care until their second trimester. Given the developmental characteristics and socialization experiences of teenagers, it is important to recognize that many of the aforementioned factors may also apply to pregnant teens.

Teen mothers also frequently experience difficulty in maintaining well-baby check-ups for their infants. Many of their difficulties can be attributed to limited maturity to handle parenthood responsibilities, limited or no support systems (i.e., family, friends, community), limited financial resources, and limited access to adequate transportation to health care facilities. For many teens, poor public transportation service in their neighborhoods alone reduces their access to clinics. Poor access to adequate transportation is also combined with lack of financial resources to obtain alternate transportation (i.e., cabs, private vehicles, etc). When teen mothers are unable to maintain regular well-baby check-ups, the infant is vulnerable to numerous health problems (i.e., rubella, polio, rickets, undetected heart, respiratory, vision, and auditory illnesses, and other infectious diseases) (Sarafino, 1990). In some cases, infants who do receive regular physical examinations and immunizations are at a greater risk of developing illnesses that can be fatal (National Commission, 1992).

For many African Americans, some very concrete problems impede their ability to maintain regular well-baby check-ups. Initially, there is the all too common lack of family support to provide the necessary guidance to ensure that the teen mother follows through with her appointments. Second, there is the sometime extreme difficulty teen mothers experience in transporting themselves and their baby to the health care facility. Finally, and strikingly, there is the teen mother's disillusionment with the services they do receive. Teen mothers waiting for long periods of time to be seen, or not being clearly told what is required of them, and appointments scheduled during school hours all compound an already complex problem (Edelman, 1987).

Much of the disillusionment experienced by African American teens regarding health care services seems as much a result of their limited knowledge about health care delivery as it is a prevailing cultural insensitivity on the part of the health care system. For example, when asked, African American teens often state they do not know what to expect when they arrive at the clinic, and frequently no one explains the process to them. These teen mothers also indicate they become impatient with the long period of waiting and leave the clinic without themselves or their babies being seen by the health care practitioner. Other African American teens state they feel health care practitioners do not understand their life styles and stresses. In addition, they perceive health care practitioners as unsympathetic to the issues they face in trying to carry out the prescribed care for their babies. While many African American teens feel their babies receive good care, their negative interpersonal interactions with the health care practitioners often further lowered their self-esteem.

The barriers confronting teen mothers in maintaining regular well-baby check-ups for their infants are not caused entirely by the health care system. These barriers are also a result of the limited supportive resources available to the teen mother. Still, such barriers dangerously impact on the health and well being of infants.

Developing good birth control practices among teen mothers to prevent subsequent unplanned pregnancies remains an ongoing problem as well. African American teens represent a higher proportion of teens who have multiple births prior to adulthood. Teen mothers that continue to have children during adolescence reduce life opportunities for themselves and their children. Specifically, research over the years suggests that multiple births to girls during adolescence increases the probability of them not completing a 12th-grade education, raising their children in poverty, and becoming dependent on social welfare programs (Brill, 1990; Edelman, 1987)—chilling life-style odds for these mothers and their children.

With such negative life styles confronting teen mothers and their children, a collaborative endeavor between the health care system, schools, and other social welfare systems is critical. It is essential for these collaborative efforts to help adolescent mothers recognize and understand how continued childbearing can negatively impact on their future.

Finally, not completing school can have devastating long-term effects on teen mothers and their babies. The absence of a high school education will reduce the teen mother's ability to function on various levels operating in contemporary society. Sadly, too, the drop out rate among teens after the birth of their babies is greatest among African Americans (Edelman, 1987).

EDUCATION

Without a minimum high school education, the mother is severely limited in the types of employment she can obtain. She becomes at risk of not being able to care for herself and her child. And the pervasiveness of this problem among African American teen mothers who do not complete their education is, again, telling (Heffernan, Shuttlesworth, & Ambrosino, 1992).

Limited education also increases a teen mother's chances of living in poverty. In the city of Norfolk, 29 percent of the children under 3 years of age live in poverty (Virginia Pilot, 1994). Even after reaching adulthood, many teen mothers find themselves and their children continuing to live in poverty and are ever dependent on social programs. The results of not completing school during their teen years become a haunting presence.

Low self-esteem is one prevailing reason for pregnant and parenting teen girls not returning to school. These teens have not gained through the various societal socialization systems (i.e., family, recreation, church, school, peer groups, etc.) avenues for developing positive self-esteem. Many of them lack a strong sense of values and skills toward developing beneficial personal goals. When present, such low self-esteem is more often reflected in their school performance than a cause of it. In the same light, and prior to their pregnancy, low self-esteem was a critical developmental factor. Often, too, becoming pregnant and their newly acquired parenting responsibilities becomes an excuse for not returning to school and completing their education. In actuality, of course, their sense of low self-esteem is the causitive factor here (Heffernan, Shuttlesworth, & Ambrosino, 1992).

Pregnant and parenting teens, for example, who have low self-esteem often feel there is little or no reason for them to return to school. They commonly also can perceive themselves as not having been good students before they became pregnant and can see, therefore, little reason to complete their education. Furthermore, these teens openly acknowledge that they become *someone* when they have a child. They perceive the baby as giving them a status, a maturity they did not possess prior to the birth. In large part, the baby defines who they are. They also feel now they have someone to love and someone who loves them.

For these teen mothers, school is often not perceived as a positive source of helping them to do or feel better. This attitude prevails largely because of their past negative experiences in school. They fail to recognize what the long-range implications of their decision not to return to school will have on their lives and their babies. Mostly, they believe, or come to believe, that everything will work out for them.

The effects here can be repetitive and cross generational. Without a minimum high school education, the mother has only limited ability to help her child succeed in school. In many instances, and despite the mother's best intentions, she projects her low self-esteem about her own education onto her child(ren), and the child(ren) suffers, in its way, the mother's loss. A negative cycle for developmental growth for the child(ren) within the family results.

Given the multitude of continued health and social conditions that are associated with adolescent pregnancy, the Commonwealth of Virginia modeled a community-based outreach program entitled "Resource Mothers Programs" that would address the issues of adolescent pregnancy. In subsequent sections of this chapter, I will discuss (1) the history of Resource Mothers Programs in Virginia, (2) Norfolk State University Resource Mothers Program, (3) accomplishments, (4) collaborative relationship between nursing and social work, and (5) implications for nursing.

HISTORY OF THE RESOURCE MOTHERS PROGRAMS IN VIRGINIA

In 1984, the Commonwealth of Virginia was facing a major health problem regarding the high incidence of teenage pregnancy, low birth weight births, infant mortality, and morbidity. Due to the magnitude of the teen pregnancy problem impacting on the poor health outcomes of mothers and infants, the then Governor Charles

S. Robb initiated a Regional Task Force on Infant Mortality, chaired by the First Lady of the Commonwealth of Virginia, Lynda Robb. As a result of its deliberations, the Task Force determined to establish "Resource Mothers Programs" in the Commonwealth of Virginia. The Resource Mothers Programs in the Commonwealth of Virginia were modeled after the program in South Carolina, which had been in existence since 1980.

The South Carolina Resource Mothers Program was enacted to decrease the dramatic increase experienced in that state of low birth weight births and infant mortality. The fundamental philosophy of the program was to provide outreach to pregnant and parenting teens. The objectives of the program were: (1) to help the mothers achieve a healthy full-term pregnancy; (2) to deliver a healthy baby; and (3) to help the mother and, when possible, the father, achieve the knowledge and capacity to provide for the developmental needs of the baby.

The Virginia Resources Mothers Programs adopted the philosophy and objectives of the South Carolina Program. This was largely due to similarities between the states in population demographics, at that time, regarding increasing rates of low birth weight births and infant mortality among teenagers in the Commonwealth.

The Norfolk State University (NSU) Resource Mothers Program, one of the original Resource Mothers Programs in Virginia, was developed in response to the growing crisis of teenage pregnancy in the City of Norfolk, with African American teenagers the largest at-risk group. The NSU Resource Mothers Program was implemented in 1985 on the campus of Norfolk State University, a natural site for the program. Norfolk State University is one of the largest historically black universities in the Commonwealth of Virginia and is among the top "five" black institutions of higher education in the nation. It has always demonstrated a strong commitment to the community and its needs. Additionally, it offers established areas of expertise in nursing, education and child development, and social work.

The implementation of the NSU Resource Mothers Program was made possible through a grant from the Virginia Department of

Health Division of Maternal and Child Health (state level), university support and the collaborative efforts of the NSU Department of Nursing, and community support from the city of Norfolk and the local Virginia Department of Health in Norfolk. In recent years, in addition to funding from the state, the program has received funding from the March of Dimes and the city of Norfolk. The program has also received in-kind support from a local health care provider in Norfolk—Sentara Health System. The NSU Resource Mothers Program has operated consistently since its inception.

NORFOLK STATE UNIVERSITY RESOURCE MOTHERS PROGRAM

Norfolk State University Resource Mothers Program and all Resource Mother Programs in the Commonwealth of Virginia operate in accordance with the objective enumerated by the U.S. Surgeon General to increase by the year 2000 the number of women who access prenatal care in the first trimester of pregnancy to 90 percent. It promotes and educates teens about accessing prenatal care early, birth control, the potentials for and the consequences of repeated pregnancies, importance of maintaining well-baby check-ups for their infants, and the significance of completing their education.

Confronting Adolescent Pregnancy: An Empowerment Model

The NSU Resource Mothers Program is designed on an empowerment model. Here, empowerment is defined as the interactive process through which individuals experience personal and social change which enables them to take action to influence and successfully engage with organizations and institutions that affect their lives (Whittmore & Kerans, 1988). The program uses the concept of "empowerment" to help teen mothers develop the personal and interpersonal skills needed to improve their life situation for themselves and their babies.

Through utilizing the underpinnings of the empowerment perspective, the program attempts to diminish the sense of powerlessness experienced by many teen mothers. Gutierre (1990) cites that females who lack access to many social resources, especially single mothers, often experienced a sense of powerlessness. Given the kinds of psychosocial contexts discussed previously in this chapter, this is particularly true for African American females and even more so for African American teen mothers.

The NSU Resource Mothers Program helps teen mothers advance beyond a sense of powerlessness and to gain some positive control over their lives. As we have seen, teen mothers experience a sense of helplessness when interacting with many formal systems, both educational and social. This is largely a result of their lack of maturity and experience to interact effectively with bureaucracies per se, especially those that structure the service delivery system. For teen mothers to gain a sense of positive control over their lives, they must begin to understand how systems operate, what resources are available, how to access resources, and what their rights are in regard to service delivery.

When focused on teens, the concept of a "sense of positive control" denotes somewhat of a conflict in U.S. society. This is primarily a result of how we view the role of teens, their place within society, and their capacity to contest it. It is imperative that society, especially service delivery systems (i.e., health, education, social welfare agencies) begin to recognize teen pregnancy and parenting as a precise social issue that requires a holistic supportive approach. With this type of approach, the service delivery system must first recognize cultural diversity and then engage in facilitation and teaching of independent, sound, and positive, decision-making skills to teens for themselves and their babies. Second, while much of society is flooded with layers of fragmented services that present many barriers to possible users, it is critical that service delivery practitioners provide direct interventions to help teen mothers increase their coping abilities and skills to support a sense of positive control. Thus enabled, teens will provide their babies with more opportunities to grow and develop in healthy and safe environments.

The pregnant and parenting teens participating in the NSU Resource Mothers Program are African American females. They are introduced to ways of managing both the micro and macro systems they must encounter in their lives (family, friends, significant others—school, health care providers, and other formal agencies). Furthermore, the program teaches teen mothers the importance of setting goals for themselves and how to enhance their inner strengths to attain their goals.

Pregnant teens have indicated that the NSU Resource Mothers Program provides support during their pregnancy by helping them understand the prescribed activities they must follow to have a healthy baby. Parenting teens also recognize that the NSU Resource Mothers Program facilitates and teaches them skills to become good parents and positive, independent decision makers on behalf of themselves and their babies. Teens state that through participation in the program they have begun to rethink their own personal goals to help improve their own and their baby's lives.

The Program Target Population

The NSU Program serves pregnant teens and teen mothers residing in the City of Norfolk Housing and Redevelopment Authority—Public Housing Developments. The public housing developments were selected as the target geographic areas because the largest proportion of African American teens reside in these neighborhoods. These housing developments also constitute a focus for high rates of teen pregnancy, low birth weight births, infant mortality, late or no prenatal care, poverty, child abuse, poor immunization of children, high rates of crime, substance abuse, sexually transmitted diseases, and poor educational achievement. The program's primary focus targets pregnant teens and teen mothers who lack knowledge, family support, and are at risk of socienvironmental factors.

Program Staff and Responsibilities

The NSU Resource Mothers Program is located and coordinated through the Department of Nursing at Norfolk State University. The program was designed by the Department of Nursing with this ongoing mission: "to assure that pregnant teens and teen mothers in the community have access to the necessary health and supportive services to assure positive outcomes for themselves and their babies" (Rice & Richardson-Collins, 1993).

The administration and service delivery staff of the programs includes: (1) a project director, (2) program coordinator, (3) outreach coordinator, (4) ten resource mothers, (5) baccalaureate nursing students, and (6) graduate social work students.

- *Project Director:* The project director is a nurse educator responsible for managing the administrative components of the program and the budget.
- *Program Coordinator:* The program coordinator is a nurse educator responsible for supervising and providing training for the resource mothers, baccalaureate nursing, and graduate social work students.
- *Outreach Coordinator:* The outreach coordinator is a social worker responsible for obtaining client referrals from health care providers, schools, and community agencies; monitoring documentation on participants; collecting data for quarterly reports; and providing information on the program.
- *Resource Mothers:* The resource mothers are the primary service providers to pregnant teens and teen mothers. Resource mothers in this program are African American women who are mothers or experienced paraprofessionals from similar socioeconomic

backgrounds as the teens participating in the program. When backgrounds are seen as similar, program participants are more accepting of the resource mother and the services she provides. The provision for resource mothers is important. Potential resource mothers are interviewed by the program coordinator for their suitability to work with pregnant and parenting teens. The extreme importance of confidentiality is stressed during the interview process.

Woman accepted as resource mothers receive a three-day orientation, 8 hours per day. Subjects presented at the orientation include: (1) immunization, (2) fetal development, (3) birth control, (4) substance abuse, (5) available community services, and (6) gaining trust and building relationships. In addition, resource mothers are required to attend continuing monthly in-service programs conducted by nursing faculty, other health care professionals, social workers, and child development specialists. The program provides the resource mother with a minimum stipend to defray the cost of transporting pregnant teens, teen mothers and their babies, and telephone expenses.

Resource mothers are responsible for:

1. Visiting teens at least once monthly with weekly monitoring as discussed during their orientation and in the home visiting guide.

2. Facilitating regular prenatal visits and well-baby checkups through providing transportation and/or companionship as needed.

3. Providing information and practical assistance for accessing community resources and activities.

4. Encouraging proper nutrition, exercise, rest, family spacing, and continuation of education.

5. Monitoring for problems related to pregnancy or child rearing practices.

6. Assisting the teen in acquiring appropriate maternal child health and social services benefits.

7. Providing support to the teen mother, her family, and the father of the baby.

Resource mothers act as lay home visitors. While the concept of lay home visiting is not a new phenomenon, it has been emphasized in this program. Quite simply, appropriate lay home visiting is a cost-effective method of delivering service to the client in her home. As lay home visitors, resource mothers promote and support health education and health protection for pregnant teens.

Throughout African American history, the grandmother has played an essential role both to her immediate and to her extended family. The grandmother provided nurturing, financial stability, and the teaching of culture and family values. With recent generational changes in many African American families, grandmothers are no longer always part of the family unit. Resource mothers have, to some degree, filled that absense, serving as a member of an extended family for many clients. They are received well by the communities they work in and by the teens they serve, prompting feelings of kinship toward them. Some teens, in fact, view them as being their grandmother. Of course, the resource mother's role is not to replace a teen's grandmother, should one not be present, but to provide support for the teen and infant. This support, via caring one-on-one relationships between the teen and resource mother, is invaluable.

Women who serve as resource mothers have strong community investments. They live in the same communities as their clients and are seen, because of their role as resource mothers, as community leaders. They provide role modeling behavior for the teen faced with issues related to pregnancy, family problems, self-esteem, and goal-setting (Rice & Richarson-Collins, 1993).

Resource mothers exemplify the *essence of caring*. They go beyond just providing basic services for their clients. They are committed to improving many of the major problems which challenge especially African American pregnant teens and teen mothers in the city of Norfolk. Some resource mothers were pregnant teens themselves and realize the benefit of having had a resource mother. Other resource mothers wished they had a resoource mother during their pregnancy and after the birth of their baby.

Resource mothers provide education, information, friendship, support, and assistance to pregnant and parenting teenagers to help foster a positive health outcome for mother and infant. These women monitor the teen mother and infant regularly to ensure that there is appropriate parent-infant bonding, that is, the teen mother's ability to establish a positive emotional and physical nurturing relationship with the baby such that the baby responds to mother as the primary caregiver. For example, teen mothers indicate that they have learned from their resource mother that an importance aspect of parent-infant bonding is the voice tone used when talking and singing to the baby, and how the baby responds to pleasant tonal qualities. Furthermore, teen mothers indicated that the program helped them to understand that the parent-infant bonding process is ongoing; they must recognize and adjust to the temperment of their babies. We must not forget, as well, that resource mothers help the teen mothers seek and receive vital appropriate community health care and social services for themselves and their babies.

Baccalaureate Nursing Students. The baccalaureate nursing students are assigned to the resource mothers program during the spring semester of each academic year. They are assigned one (1) case, a pregnant teen, for sixteen (16) weeks.

Nursing students are responsible for:

1. Home visits to the teen on a weekly basis for 16 weeks.
2. Providing the teen with intense health education about their pregnancy and how to care for their baby.
3. Reinforcing the instructions given to the teen by the health care provider.

4. Monitoring the teen for signs and symptoms of possible complications during pregnancy.

The nursing students work closely with the resource mothers and social work students to provide necessary information about the condition of the teen.

Graduate Social Work Students. The graduate social work students are assigned to the program for one (1) academic year. They are assigned 10 cases to provide social work intervention on an ongoing basis. The social work students serves in the role as case managers.

Social work students are responsible for:

1. Establishing a professional working relationship with the teen, family members, and significant others (i.e., baby's father and peers) in the home through regular home visits.
2. Assessing the teen's level of compliance in following health care providers instructions.
3. Assessing the family's behavior to support the teen during the pregnancy and after the birth of the baby.
4. Assessing the teen's school attendance and follow-up with school officials.
5. Providing counseling sessions with teen regarding issues she may have, the family, or as a result of identified problems by the social work student.
6. Working with the teen mother and the baby's father, if possible, to identify needs she and the baby may have, and establish a contract with them.
7. Networking with health care providers, department of social services, schools, and child care providers to help teen mothers learn how to access necessary services.

8. Maintaining communication with resources mothers, nursing students, and the program coordinator regarding the teen's physical and mental health.

The social work students provide the program with clinical services and community resource networking.

ACCOMPLISHMENTS

The NSU Resource Mothers Program has been an effective method for helping pregnant and parenting teens in Norfolk, Virginia; positive outcomes are the norm for participants served. As the primary component of the program, resource mothers demonstrate positive attitudes and commitment to the teens and provide excellent services. The program continues to use a variety of marketing strategies to be successful in reaching pregnant and parenting teens.

The program utilizes baccalaureate nursing and graduate social work students to expose these future professionals to the issues of adolescent pregnancy and the importance of grass roots work in the community. Through a collaborative effort between nursing and social work, the program provides a holistic approach to service delivery for pregnant and parenting teens.

State Results

The state results confirm the success of Resource Mothers Programs. Teens who participate in the program have better pregnancy outcomes. Low birth weight births for program participants was 7.3 compared to 11.0 percent of all births to teenagers. The infant mortality rate for program participants was 6.9 per 1,000 live births. Two-thirds of the program participants returned to school.

And, of the total population served, 80 percent of them postponed a repeat pregnancy (Virginia Department of Health, 1992).

Norfolk State University Resource Mothers Program Results

Of the 152 project participants from January 1, 1991, through March 30, 1993, only 11 of the infants born weighed less than 2500 grams. There was only one infant death. Of the total project participants (n = 152), 122 have remained in or graduated from school (Rice & Richardson-Collins, 1993).

COLLABORATIVE RELATIONSHIP BETWEEN NURSING AND SOCIAL WORK

The professions of nursing and social work have a rich history of community-based service. In recognizing how environmental systems impact on the functioning of the population served, social work practice offers to the program a comprehensive approach to helping teens and their families cope more effectively with the challenges facing them. Though utilizing social work students, the program has also increased its linkages and networking between community systems that can be of assistance to pregnant and parenting teens. It has allowed the program to take a more problem-solving approach that integrates the psychological, social, and physiological needs of teens. Counseling with the teen, family members, and significant others by social work students has afforded more intense opportunities to increase positive outcomes for all concerned. The collaboration between nursing and social work has allowed the NSU Resource Mothers Program to become a unique and comprehensive service provider in reducing the problems associated with adolescent pregnancy.

IMPLICATIONS FOR NURSING

Leininger (1986) describes caring as the "essence of nursing." The profession of nursing has long demonstrated the caring concept. Nursing interventions, expertise, theory, and intuition all advance greater understanding for the client and significant others. The profession of nursing has also been using the lay home visitors concept for many years. Committed to an expansive, ongoing style of interventions, nursing is able to extract, disseminate, and intervene appropriately. Here, the special ability of the nurse to utilize intuition as a way of understanding expands the boundaries of intervention and enhances client and caregiver rapport. In this light, the NSU Department of Nursing is providing a nontraditional, culturally diverse clinical experience for its unique student population.

Baccalaureate nursing and graduate social work students are finding the Norfolk State University Resource Mothers Program experience an essential component in understanding the delivery of care to a culturally diverse adolescent population. Documentation from students, clients, and resource mothers support the need for this community-based approach, the "Resource Mothers Program."

REFERENCES

Bernstein, R. (1982). *Helping unmarried mothers.* New York: Association Press.

Brill, N. (1990). *Working with people: The helping process.* 4th ed. New York: Longmans.

Edelman, M. W. (1987). *Families in peril: An agenda for social change.* Cambridge: Harvard University Press.

Ell, K., & Northen, H. (1990). *Families and health care: Psychosocial practice.* New York: Aldine.

Garzon, L., & Benjamin-Coleman, R. (1993). Factors associated with delayed prenatal care. *Program of Sigma Theta Tau International Meeting*. Madrid, Spain.

Gutierre, L. (March 1990). Working with women of Color: An empowerment Perspective. *Social Work, 35*(2), 149–153.

Heffernan, J., Shuttlesworth, G. & Ambrosino, R. (1992). *Social work and social welfare an introduction*. 2nd ed., St. Paul, MN: West.

Leininger, M. M. (1986). Care facilitation and resistance factors in the culture of nursing. *Transcultural Nursing, 8*(3), 1–12

National Commission to Prevent Infant Mortality. (March 1992). Troubling trends persist: Short change America's next generation. Washington, DC: Author.

Rice, R., & Richardson-Collins, A. M. (1993) Resource mothers as lay health providers. *Program of Sigma Theta Tau International Meeting*. Madrid, Spain.

Sarafino, E. (1990). *Health psychology: Biopsychosocial interactions*. New York: Wiley.

Staff. (April, 1994). A quiet crisis. *The Virginia Pilot,* Section D.

Stanhope, M., & Lancaster, J. (1992). *Community health nursing: Process and practice for promoting health*. Philadelphia, PA: Mosby.

State of Virginia. (1992). *Annual statistical report.*

Virginia Department of Maternal Child Health. (1993). *Program statistical report,* Richmond, Virginia.

Whittmore, E., & Kerans, P. (1988). Participation, empowerment, and welfare. *Canadian Review of Social Policy. 22,* 51–60.

Chapter Six

African American Family Resources for Coping: The Dance of Stress

Bertha L. Davis

For many years, the African American family has been the focus of research studies. Studies reveal that a gap in health status between African Americans and other groups is continuing to widen. In this chapter, while I do not purport to identity an exhaustive array of strategies for determining stress, and intervening in and managing stressful situations, I do challenge healthcare professionals involved in the facilitation of health and well being of African American families to provide an awareness of selected resources that have been found significant.

DEFINITION OF STRESS

I have adapted the present stress, or dance of stress, analysis from an important study on anger by Lerner (1985), who provides a guide based on Bowen's Family System theory for change in patterns of intimate relationships. Additionally, Lerner presents an analysis of anger based upon what she describes as challenges; old, new, and countermoves; circular dances; triangles; and generational transmission. Her analysis provides an excellent parallel for analyzing stress and stress response.

According to the National Center for Health Statistics, blacks continue to comprise the largest minority group in the United

States, approximately 12 percent of the general population. Appreciably higher proportions of blacks experience proportionately higher numbers of health problems over other minorities in many areas. Although stress is not a problem only among African Americans, it does present a substantial presence in family functioning among African Americans. Family use of a variety of problem-solving styles also suggests that families have a repertoire of strategies to establish and maintain equilibrium when stress occurs. Because African Americans are exposed to a range of stressors (Folkman, 1984), they need effective methods to reduce stress and enhance both individual and family adaptation.

Throughout the literature on family interaction, stress is seen in various ways. Stress theory, for example, delineates the concept based upon definitions, states, and outcomes. Miller-Keane (1992, p. 1422) defines stress as the sum of biological reactions to any adverse stimuli—physical, mental, or emotional, internal or external—that tends to disturb the homeostasis of an organism, and the stimuli that elicit reactions. Stressors are any factors that disturb homeostasis, producing stress (p. 1423). Stress, then, is a signal that system balance is being challenged or has the potential to be challenged. And coping is a process of contending with life's difficulties in an effort to overcome them (p. 355). The question of how a family actually does cope with the stressors that disturb it is of great import.

Negative perception of families, inadequate resources, ineffective problem solving, and lack of family support are all stressors commonly felt within the family. Effective coping here, at least according to Miller-Keane (1992), may require strategies to improve self-concept, build self-esteem, and establish an appropriate reward structure for family members to identify more healthy ways to cope.

The moves by which families collectively protect themselves and prevent over- and underfunctioning reinforces patterns of stress response. The types of patterns—circular, triangular, and so forth—in which families find themselves can be either productive or nonproductive based on the most familiar outcomes that establish the pattern, with functional response considered a coping behavior and dysfunctional response a stressful behavior.

WHY STUDY AFRICAN AMERICAN FAMILIES

The responses of African Americans are most understood when analyzed over time and in concert with developmental processes that have formed their basic personality patterns. Understanding the presenting biological, psychological, social, cultural, political, and spiritual factors as they relate to reactions, interactions, and critical incidents enables one to ferret out the role perceptions, resources, and desires that are impacted by interventions for the person in an environment that establishes behavioral patterns and subsequent conditioned responses.

Modes of awareness, as based on data gleaned from experiences and perceptions of other human capacities of awareness, enables us to bring meaning to our lives and the world, both psychological and physical, of which we live (Munhall & Boyd, 1993). Because the self and our world are socially constructed, so are our changing processes of interaction. Understanding of behavioral response occurs, then, in social, situational, and interactional contexts. This transactional system, which allows for examining actions and interactions in relationship to conditions and consequences, operates reflective of a conditioned response of stress and/or coping. As we attempt to make adaptations, a denial and defense mechanism may also become operational (Strauss & Corbin, 1990). Fortunately, as a response to stress, denial is not always negative (Lazarus, 1991). What denying does promulgate in terms of behavior and prognosis in the treatment process, however, needs to be explored.

Specifically, this treatment process comprises the effort by health care providers to discover maladaptive patterns that may or may not infer underlying causes of behavior. A recognition presides that it is not essential to just extinguish old behaviors and replace them with new behaviors, but to maintain ongoing assessment and identify techniques for teaching coping strategies. These strategies should be explored in view of current family characteristics and environmental stimuli that reinforce adaptive behavior. An understanding of discrete adaptive behaviors exchanged among family members, antecedent factors, and interactional consequences are far more important than the cerebral conclusions of health care providers who view certain responses as dysfunctional. In every situation that produces stress in the African American family, the relationships between health status, social roles, and cultural factors which impact those situations must be explored. A holistic focus is needed vis-á-vis strategies that focus on broader issues of race, gender, class, self-concept, and other historical views and psychodynamics of what it means to be African American in the world today.

Any survey of the literature regarding the health status of African American families would support the fact that disparity exists as well as proposing answers about how best to apply interventions (teaching, counseling, screening, and so on) to improve quality-of-life while allowing for cultural differences. There are unanswered questions about who are appropriate providers, who should be available to provide certain services, and what services are needed. As quality of life issues are analyzed for all Americans, data continue to support disparities regarding the health status of African Americans. As such, there is great need to describe and interpret the African American family as it emerges in today's health care arena. The economic forces alone impacting the African American family are also of unprecedented proportions. Certainly, to facilitate understanding of the African American family as it confronts the forces that have shaped patterns over the centuries requires that we seize upon the appropriate contemporary and theoretical perspectives.

A lack of theories appropriate to the family in general is one reason for the paucity of theories specific to the African American family. Although a rationale for theory development regarding families has been established through the development of a family conceptual framework using descriptive taxonomic models (Hill, 1958; Hill, Reiss, & Nye, 1979), this still does satisfy our need. Many existing frameworks have only occasionally been used in research on African Americans. Often, the analysis of ethnic and lower-class families within the context of these frameworks has required truncation or stretching of data to accommodate the theoretical realities posed by them (Staples & Johnson, 1993).

In 1979, McAdoo conducted a study to determine the levels of stress and family support in African American families. McAdoo explored the presence of stress in a group of African American families with school age children and those who moved up to middle-class status. Through the use of several instruments—the Holmes and Rahe Schedule of Life Events to measure levels of stress and the Standard Happiness Scale to measure satisfaction with life—McAdoo ascertained that 52 percent of African American participants, who were acutely aware of the impact of racism on their lives and their children, felt satisfied with their family. In this regard, the results of McAdoo's and similar studies indicated the need for additional research in the areas of family functioning of African Americans as well as the need to integrate social-environmental characteristics and perception of family interaction into theories of family stress and coping. The integration of these variables into theories devoted to analyzing family stress and coping mechanisms would also serve as logical extensions to existing theories of family stress and coping.

Some of the advantages of using information about family functioning in ongoing therapy situations and having the knowledge of such include being able to: (1) structure and focus therapy sessions, (2) enhance the probability of more balanced discussion since each family member's views would be represented, and (3) identify similarities of perceptions and ideals leading to an incentive for family members to work productively on shared areas of dissatisfaction (Moos, 1981a). The Family Environment Scale (FES) encourages a clear, practical focus on family members' perception of the family environment. In addition, repeated assessments can be undertaken to monitor progress in family therapy situations and to indicate whether goals have changed and a new consensus attained (Moos, 1981b).

Studies on the African American family will add to the research on African American families and to research methodologies in family processes by using a family level of analysis in both the theoretical and statistical treatment of the data. Furthermore, agreement scores between African American family members, as a family-level consensus variable, would reveal for all families domains of social-environmental dimensions that could be used as predictors of the coping ability of the African American family and their hardiness. Additionally, exploration of the relationship between the definition of the stressor events and resources with coping behaviors in African American family members should be pursued. The first significant need of such an investigation would be to link selected African American family social environmental characteristics to the family's ability to cope with stress. In this light, McCubbin (1980) describes a need for studies on factors that assist families, in this instance, African American families, in adjusting to and avoiding the impact of stressor events, and for studying factors such as coping, family resources, and relationships. Most recently, as well, McCubbin et al. (1995) has added resiliency to the study of phenomena of concern. Resiliency is wide ranging and alludes to factors such as coherence and spirituality as variables in recovery.

THEORETICAL CONSIDERATIONS IN FAMILY RESEARCH

As early as 1936, Angell made the first systematic analysis of factors that were related to the ability of families to cope with stress, such as integration and adaptability, in effect, the family resources, and particularly as they defined social and environmental characteristics (Moos, 1976). In 1978, Pearlin and Schooler identified three personal psychological resources residing within the self which can reduce the stressful consequences of social strain: (1) self-esteem—the positiveness of attitude toward self; (2) self-denigration—the extent and effect of negative attitudes toward self; and (3) mastery—the sometime fatalistically ruled, psychological resources most efficacious to family members facing strains arising out of conditions over which they felt they had little direct control. This assumption by Pearlin and Schooler that personal resources can reduce stress is consistent with McCubbin's (1979) assertion that the quality of interpersonal relationships, along with group support and clear community norms, enhances the family's ability to cope.

In 1988, McAdoo, as did McCubbin in 1980, indicated the need for studies that assist African American families in adjusting to the impact of stressor events. As a result, my own examination of African American family resources, specifically, social-environmental characteristics that either facilitate or hinder their coping abilities, became even more significant. Having limited previous investigations to the social environmental characteristics of cohesion, expressiveness, conflict, independence, achievement orientation, intellectual-cultural orientation, active recreational orientation, moral religious emphasis, organization, and control, I found these characteristics to be related to coping as well. Additionally, literature reveals that stress increases as environmental factors have pile-up effects (McCubbin & McCubbin, 1988).

HILL'S ABCX MODEL

Hill's ABCX (Hill, 1949, 1958, 1971) model of families experiencing stress was the conceptual framework undergirding my most recent study on coping strategies used by African American families experiencing stress. This horizontal building approach was undertaken to increase the pool of data on selected aspects of African American family resources for coping with stress and it also provided the means to pool other aspects of data for analysis. This approach provided a means for ascertaining descriptions of personal growth and interpersonal relationships among family members, with data focused on future research initiatives toward the discovery of therapeutic family interventions. These interventions included methods to maintain appropriate levels of family functioning, behaviors that show respect and empathy, and utilization of methods of confrontation, self-disclosure, and catharsis to enhance personal growth. Independence, achievement orientation, intellectual-cultural orientation, active-recreational orientation, and an emphasis on moral-religious values can all significantly affect personal growth as well.

Simply put, Hill's ABCX model postulates that (A) stressor events interact with (B) the family's resources for coping and (C) with the family's perception of the event and status they ascribe to it. Taken together, they produce or extenuate (X) the crisis at hand. According to McCubbin (1980), absent from this conceptual model, and which should be included, is coping behavior. As a result, I concluded that satisfactory coping behavior would decrease the likelihood of stressful crisis-oriented events which, if allowed to continue, could very well lead to a more general state of crisis in the African American family per se. Here, the coping ability of African American family members was assumed to relate directly and positively to the family's social-environmental characteristics (Olsen, 1979, 1983) (see Figure 1).

As revised for a second study, the (X) component in the Hill ABCX model, referring to crisis and coping strategies, was substituted for the crisis component only. This study addressed the proposition that the family's social-environmental characteristics, in existence at the time that the stressor events occur, would influence coping behaviors initiated after events had occurred. In this light, coping behavior was considered a dependent variable. I also proposed a relationship between (B) and (C) components. For example, the family's definition of the event's seriousness would be influenced by family resources. Here, I viewed family resources as prerequisites for establishing effective coping strategies. Therefore, the family's social-environmental characteristics available at the time the stressor event occurs would influence coping behaviors initiated after events had occurred.

The subsequent conceptual framework integrated major aspects of individual (Pearlin & Schooler, 1978) and family approaches to the study of stress and coping (Hill 1949, 1971; McCubbin et al., 1980). In this conceptual framework, the family's ability to cope becomes a function of two intervening variables/family resources: social-environmental characteristics and the family's definitions of the stressor events. In this regard, I suggest a direct relationship between the amount of emotional distress experienced by family members subsequent to the event and its direct impact on individual African American family members' permissiveness, conflict, independence, achievement orientation, intellectual cultural orientation, and active recreational orientation.

In a recent review of the literature, McCubbin (1980) further asserts that the preponderance of family research is based on Hill's ABCX model, but that additional research is needed to test the specific assumptions of the model, for example, the impact of the family's perception of social-environmental characteristics, stressor events, and changes in the likelihood of a family crisis occurring.

OPERATIONALIZATION OF MODEL

In an effort to operationalize Hill's ABCX conceptual framework, as modified by McCubbin, several variables were delineated. *Independent variables* include the (A) component of the conceptual framework—the stressor event. Stressors, defined as those life events that are of sufficient influence to impose change on the family system, were assessed to determine individual African American family members' perceptions of the impact of the change event on the entire family (Hill, 1949; McCubbin et al., 1980). The (B) component of the model also consisted of the following independent

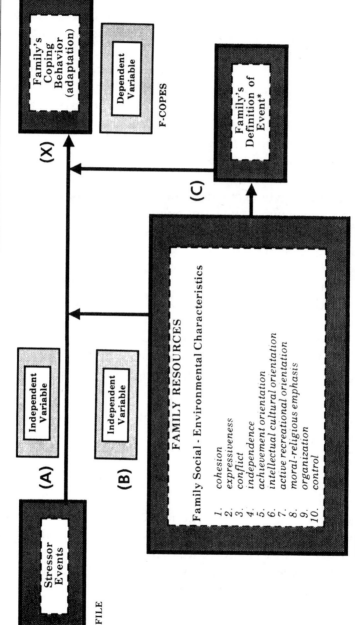

Figure 1
Research Theoretical Framework

Stressor Events
FILE

(A)
Independent Variable

(B)
Independent Variable

FAMILY RESOURCES
Family Social - Environmental Characteristics

1. cohesion
2. expressiveness
3. conflict
4. independence
5. achievement orientation
6. intellectual cultural orientation
7. active recreational orientation
8. moral-religious emphasis
9. organization
10. control

FES

(X)

Family's Coping Behavior (adaptation)

Dependent Variable

F-COPES

(C)

Family's Definition of Event*

variables: family resources delineated as family characteristics, such as cohesion, expressiveness, conflict, independence, achievement orientation, intellectual cultural orientation, active recreational orientation, moral-religious emphasis, organization, and control, were defined as social-environmental characteristics that either increase or decrease the family's ability to respond to stressor events. The (C) component of the framework consisted of the family's definition of the event. As conceptualized by Hill (1958), this construct acknowledges the fact that all families will not perceive the same events as stressful or as having the same degree of stress and, therefore, the amount of hardship caused by stressor events will vary across families. Perception of events take on an added dimension when analyzed in the context of coping; the normative and non-normative events include perception as a critical factor in determining severity of the stressor event (McCubbin et al., 1980). The difference between events which eventually lead to breakdown or dysfunction may depend upon the presence or absence of explanations which assist the family in understanding what has occurred and why, and how the environment can be rearranged to overcome the unwanted experience. Therefore, an analysis of coping has to take into account the different types of meaning engendered by the family which enable continued functioning despite the presence of the stressor event. Some researchers have even gone so far as to assign weights to specific life events which indicate the relative amount of hardship caused by stressor events (Stone, 1971). Weighing norms will provide an objective appraisal of the severity of the stressor event and identify families by the definition of the event as compared to national norms: (1) more severe, (2) less severe, and (3) equally. Coping behavior comprised the *dependent* variable (X) of the model. Coping was measured by investigation of dependent variables such as level of coping response, adequacy of coping behaviors, and number of coping behaviors, and social-environmental characteristics that influence family coping responses. Here, the more coping behaviors utilized, the less amount of stress caused by the life events, the greater number of individuals involved. The congruence between real and ideal responses to stressor events can reveal adequacy of coping. Cognitive coping strategies referred to ways in which individual family members changed their subjective perceptions of stressful situations. This perspective focused on individual family members and their psychological state and subjective-psychological bridge to family stress, which then became a process of achieving balance in the family system to facilitate comparable patterning and promote individual growth and development. Figure 2 presents a process criterion for cognitive health behavior.

Assessment of family members' perceptions of their family environment along social-environmental dimensions of relationship, personal growth, and family maintenance further focus our attention on communication and interaction patterns. Moos (Moos & Moos, 1981) family environment scale (FES) provides data on social climate that reflects family members efforts to convey stress and need for support.

RELIGIOUS SOCIALIZATION

Private religious notions have an impact on family responses (see Figure 3). Preliminary qualitative findings from interviews with African American family members reflect that the magnitude of spiritual belief does have an impact on stress levels. The statistical significance, if any, however, is unknown and in further studies this author will continue to explore the issue. Religious affiliation seems to establish a network that serves to undergird a faith that maintains belief at a level in which one can cope satisfactorily. Other institutions that are a vital force in the African American community include school, business, and government. Within all institutions, it is important to know the appropriate interventions to utilize when responding to the needs of African American families and every ethnic group. Gary (1991) articulates notions she has gleaned from African American researchers which describe what is called a "world view." She further selects concepts of groupness and commonality of purpose, cooperation and collective responsibility, cooperation and independence, survival of the tribe, oneness in nature, and experiential approaches to life as factors to be considered. Further, primary providers in our culture should develop theoretical and practical content and become more sensitive to historic, economic, political, social, and cultural factors associated with institutional racism and overall functioning to include the health and welfare of African Americans (Gary, 1991; Tucker-Allen, 1991; Giger & Davidnizar, 1991). Additionally, despite many factors and hardships experienced by the African American family, it has remained strong and powerful in the lives of black people. Here, kinship structures have been a key in holding the family together.

However, according to Blackwell (1991), second only to the family, the church is still the most important social institution in the black community. Blackwell also identified seven functions of the contemporary black church: (1) it provides a cohesive institutional structure within the black community; (2) it is an instrument for the development of black leadership; (3) it is a basis for citizenship training and community social action; (4) it performs major educative and social roles; (5) it acts as a charitable institution; (6) it is an agency for the development of black business structure in ventures; and (7) it serves as an index of social class. This role is especially critical at a time when the African American family has undergone a transformation as evidenced by problems like poverty and inadequate health care that plague society. The church stresses family values and responsibility, and there is still a tendency for the African American community to utilize the church to gain direction and psychological support and coping strategies for dealing with stressors of everyday existence. The history of the church in America reveals an immense religious diversity within the African American community. Of special significance here are the

Figure 2
Cognitive Health Behavior Criterion

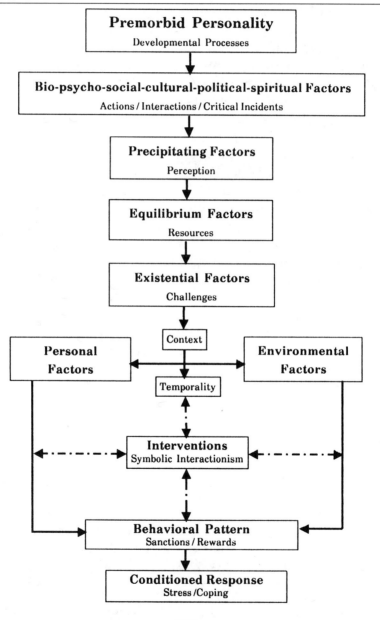

Figure 3
Schematic of Spiritual-Titre Development

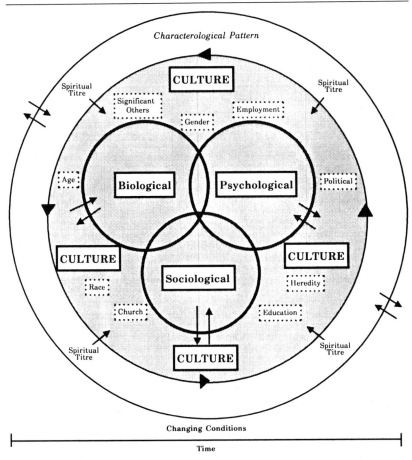

Spiritual Titre is represented by degree(s) of shaded area. This legend represents levels of spiritual titre within individuals.

High Titre   Medium Titre   Low Titre

bonds forged by the church toward a sense of community that remains a vital force currently and continuously shared by African Americans (Blackwell, 1991).

CONCLUSION

The family unit has become increasingly important as a resource for problem solving; however, current pressures on families are difficult to assess. In the case of the African American family, the data are even less replete with scales that adequately reflect the family member's ability to cope with stressful events and adapt successfully to them. Research is significant to the nursing discipline because it has the potential for explaining health phenomena and guiding nursing practice in clinical settings where the family is an integral part of the intervention. The use of family stress theory is especially relevant in promoting health during normal family transitions, and in assessing family changes during a family member's period of stress or experiences with stressors. Certainly, more studies with implications for generating pertinent data on and about African American families across the life-span and their resources used for coping are needed.

Recently, there are signs of a spirit of renewal among African American families and family members. Both are a result of family-community bonds and development of individual and collective spiritual resources. Although the family is one of the main agents for the transmission of ethics, values, and religious traditions, family scholars have, for the most part, ignored these issues in family research (Boss et al., 1993). Basic qualitative approaches have given life to data by capturing conceptions of a process analytically which is more than a cursory allusion and offers the possibility of more in-depth examinations of data. Within this context, the resiliency of the African American family and family members is something to behold.

REFERENCES

Angell, R. (1936). *The family encounters depression*. New York: Scribner.

Bachrach, C. A. (1980, August). Childlessness and social isolation among the elderly. *Journal of Marriage and the Elderly, 51*, 627–637.

Barnfather, J. S., & Lyon, B. (1993). *Stress and coping*. Indianapolis, IN: Center of Nursing Press of Sigma Theta Tau International.

Benbenishty, R. (1991). *Combat stress reaction and changes in military medical profile*. Dallas, TX: Association of Military Surgeons of U.S., 69–70.

Bernheim, C., Pruitt, R. H., & Tomlinson, J. Pitt. (1991). *Military medicine*. Dallas, TX: Association of Military Surgeons of U.S., 51–53.

Blackwell, J. E. (1991). *The black community*. New York: HarperCollins.

Bolin, R., & Klenow, D. J. (1988). Older people in disaster: A comparison of black and white victims. *International Journal of Aging and Human Development, 26*, 29–43.

Bowen, M. (1978). *Family therapy in clinical practice*. New York: Aronson.

Boss, P., Doherty, W., LaRossa, R., Schumm, W., & Steinmetz, S. (1993). *Sourcebook of family theories and methods*. New York: Plenum Press.

Braithwaite, R., & Taylor, S. (1992). *Health issues in the black community*. San Francisco, CA: Jossey-Bass.

Brophy, M H. (1991). *Cyproheptadine for combat nightmares in posttraumatic stress disorder and dream anxiety disorder*. Dallas, TX: Association of Military Surgeons of U.S.

Bryant, Z. L., & Coleman, M. (1988). The black family as portrayed in introductory family textbooks. *Family Relations, 37*, 255–259.

Burr, W. R. (1982). *Theory constructive and the sociology of the family*. New York: Wiley.

Centerwall, B. S. (1984). Race, socio-economic status and domestic homicide, Atlanta 1971–72. *American Journal of Public Health, 74*, 831–851.

Cronkite, R., & Moos, R. (1980). The determinants of post treatment functioning of alcoholic patients: A conceptual framework. *Journal of Consulting and Clinical Psychology, 48*, 305–316.

Conner-Edwards, A. S., & Spurlock, J. (1988). *Black families in crises: The middle class.* New York: Brunner/Mazel.

Conway, K. (1985). Coping with the stress of medical problems among black and white elderly. *International Journal of Aging and Human Development, 2,* 39–47.

Dancy, B., & Handal, P. (1980) Perceived family climate of black adolescents: A function of parental marital status on perceived conflict. *Journal of Community Psychology, 8,* 208–214.

Danielson, C. B., Hamel-Bissell, B., & Winstead-Fry, P. (1993). *Families, health, & illness.* St. Louis: Mosby.

Davis, B., Hammond, P., & Montgomery, A. (1993). Developing a career trajectory. *ABNF Journal* (4)*4,* 101–103.

Davis, B., Daniel, E., & Sloan, P. (1993). Research notes. *ABNF Journal,* (4)4–105.

Dilworth-Anderson, P., & McAdoo, H. P. (1988). The Study of ethnic minority families: Implications for practitioners and policy makers. *Family Relations, 37,* 265–267.

Dressler, W. (1985). The social and cultural context of coping: Action, gender and symptoms in a southern Black community. *Social Science and Medicine, 21,* 499–506.

Fowler, P. (1980). Family environment and early behavioral development: A structural analysis of dependencies. *Psychological Reports, 47,* 611–617.

Gary, F., & Kavanaugh, C. (1991). *Psychiatric mental health nursing.* Philadelphia: J.B. Lippincott.

Guidubaldi, J., & Cleminshaw, H. (1985). Divorce, family health and child adjustment. *Family Relations, 34,* 35–41.

Giger, J., & Davidhizar, R. (1991) *Transcultural nursing: Assessment and intervention.* St.Louis: Mosby.

Goldenberg, I., C. J., & Goldenberg, H. (1991). *Family therapy overview.* 3rd Ed. Pacific Grove, CA: Brooks/Cole.

Hill, R. (1949). *Families under stress.* New York: Harper Publishers.

Hill, R. (1958). Social stresses on the family. *Social Casework, 49,* 139–158.

Hill, R. B. (1971). *The strengths of black families.* 2nd ed. New York: National Urban League.

Hill, R. & Reiss, D. & Nye, I. (1979). *Contemporary theories about the family: Volume I.* New York: New York Press.

Hymovich, D. P., & Baker, C. D. (1985). The needs, concerns and coping of parents with cystic fibrosis. *Family Relations, 34,* 91–97.

Joynes, G., Davis, & Williams, R. H., Jr. (Eds.) (1989). *A common destiny: Blacks and American society.* Washington, DC: National Academy Press.

Krueger, J. C., Nelson, A., & Walanin, M. (1988). *Nursing research: Development, collaboration, and utilization.* Rockville, Maryland: Aspen Systems Corporation.

Lazarus, R. S. (1991). *Emotion and adaption.* New York: Oxford University Press.

Lazarus, R., & Folkman, S. (1984). *Stress appraisal, and coping.* New York: Spring Publishers.

Lavee, Y. (1985). Family types and family adaptation to stress: Integrating the circumplex model of family systems and the family adjustment and adaptation response model. Unpublished Doctoral Dissertation. *Dissertation Abstracts International,* University of Minnesota, St. Paul.

Leininger, M. (1991). A theory of nursing. In M. Leininger (Ed.), *The theory of culture care diversity and universality.* New York: National League for Nursing.

Lerner, H. G. (1985). *The dance of anger.* New York: Harper & Row.

McAdoo, H. P. (1977). *The impact of extended family variables upon the upward mobility of black families.* Columbia, MD: Columbia Research Systems.

McAdoo, H. P. (1978). Factors related to stability in upwardly mobile black families. *Journal of Marriage and Family, 40,* 761–776.

McAdoo, H. P. (1979). Black kinship. *Psychology Today, 12,* 64.

McAdoo, J. (1979). Father-child interaction patterns and self-esteem in black school children. *Young Children, 34,* 46–53.

McAdoo, H. P. (1988). *Black families.* 2nd ed. Newbury Park, CA: Sage.

Mays, R. M. (1988). Family stress and adaptation. *Nurse Practitioner, 8,* 52–56.

McCubbin, H. I., Thompson, E. A., Thompson, A. I., & Fromer, J. E. (1995). *Sense of coherence and resiliency* Madison, WI: The University of Wisconsin System.

McCubbin, H. I. (1979). Integrating coping behavior in family stress. *The Journal of Marriage and the Family, 41,* 237–244.

McCubbin, H. I., Cauble, E., & Patterson, J. (1982). *Family stress, coping and social support.* Springfield, IL: Charles C. Thomas.

McCubbin, H. I., & Dahl, B. (1985). *Marriage and family: Individuals and life cycles.* New York: Wiley.

McCubbin, H. I., & McCubbin, M. A. (1988). Topologies of resilient families: Emerging roles of social class and ethnicity. *Family Relations,* 247–254.

McCubbin, H. I., McCubbin, M. A., Patterson, J. M., Cauble, A. E., Wilson, L. R., & Warrick, W. (1983). CHIP - Coping Health Inventory for Parents: An assessment of parental coping patterns in the case of the chronically ill child. *Journal of Marriage and the Family,* 359–370.

McCubbin, H. I., Needle, R. H., & Wilson, M. (1985). Adolescent health risk behavior: Family stress and adolescent coping as critical factors. *Family Relations, 34.*

McCubbin, H. I., & Patterson, J. M. (1982). Family adaptation to crises. In H. McCubbin, A. Cauble, & J. Patterson (Eds.), *Family stress, coping and social support,* pp. 26–47. Springfield, IL: Charles C. Thomas.

McCubbin, H. I., & Patterson, J. M. (1983). Family stress and adaptation to crises: A double ABCX model of family behavior. In D. Olson & B. Miller (Eds.), *Family studies review yearbook.* Beverly Hills, CA: Sage.

McCubbin, H. I., & Patterson, J. M. (1983). The family stress process: The double ABCX model of family adjustment and adaptation. In H. McCubbin, M. Sussman, & Jim Patterson (Eds.), *Advances and development in family stress theory and research,* pp. 7–37. New York: Haworth.

McCubbin, H. I., & Patterson, J. M. (1983). Stress: The family inventory of life events and changes. In E. Filsinger (Ed.), *A sourcebook of marriage and family assessment,* pp. 275–297. Beverly Hills, CA: Sage.

McCubbin, H. I., Patterson, J. M., & Wilson, L. (1979). *File family inventory of life events and changes, Form A.* (Research Instrument). St. Paul, MN: University of Minnesota.

McCubbin, H. I., Patterson, J. M., & Wilson, L. (1981). *File—Form C.* St. Paul, MN: University of Minnesota.

McCubbin, M. A. (1988). Family stress, resources, and family types: Chronic illness in children. *Family Relations, 37,* 203–210.

Miller-Keane (1992). *Encyclopedia & dictionary of medicine, nursing, & allied health.* 5th ed. Philadelphia: W.B. Saunders.

Mishel, M. H., (1984). Perceived uncertainty and stress in illness. *Research in Nursing and Health, 7,* 163–171.

Mitchell, R. E., Cronkite, R. C., & Moos, R. H. (1983). Stress, coping and depression among marriage couples. *Journal of Abnormal Psychology, 92,* 433–438.

Moos, R. (1976). A typology of family social environments. *Family Process, 15,* 357–370.

Moos, R., & Moos, B. (1981). *Family environment scale manual.* Los Angeles, CA: Consulting Psychologist Press, Inc.

Moos, R. (1976). A typology of family social environments. *Family Process, 15,* 357–370.

Moos, R., Bromet, E., Tsu, V., & Moos, B. (1979). Family characteristics and the outcome of treatment for alcoholism. *Journal of Studies on Alcohol, 40,* 78–88.

Moos, R., & Moos, B. (1981a). *The process of recovery from alcoholism II. Comparing family functioning in alcoholic and matched control families.* Social Ecology Laboratory, Stanford University, and Veterans Administration Medical Center, Palo Alto, CA.

Moos, R., & Moos, B. (1981b). *Family environment scale manual.* California: Consulting Psychologist Press, Inc.

Munhall, P. L., & Boyd, C. O. (1993). *Nursing research: A qualitative perspective.* New York: National League for Nursing Press.

National Caucus and Center on Black Aged, for the Select Committee on Aging, U.S. House of Representatives. (1987). *The status of the black elderly in the United States,* Committee Publication No. 100–622: Washington, DC: Government Printing Office.

Newcomb, M., Huba, G., & Bentler, P. (1986). Desirability of various life change events among adolescents: Effects of exposure, sex, age, and ethnicity. *Journal of Research in Personality,* 207–227.

Neal, A. M., & Turner, S. M. (1991). *Anxiety disorders research with African Americans: Current status.* Ohio: American Psychological Association, Inc.

Nyamath, A. (1989). Comprehensive health seeking and coping paradigm. *Journal of Advanced Nursing, 24,* 281–290.

Olson, D. H. (1983). *Families: What makes them work.* Beverly Hills, CA: Sage.

Olson, D., Sprenkle, D., & Russell, C. (1979). Circumplex model of marital and family systems I: Cohesion and adaptability dimensions, family types and clinical applications. *Family Process, 18,* 3–28.

Olson, D. H., Russell, C. S., Sprenkle, D. H., (1983). Circumplex Model VI: Theoretical update. *Family Process, 22,* 69–83.

Patterson, J. M. (1985). Critical factors affecting family compliance with home treatment for children with cystic fibrosis. *Family Relations, 34,* 79–89.

Patterson, J. M., & McCubbin, H. I. (1984). Gender roles and coping. *Journal of Marriage and the Family,* 95–104.

Pearlin, L., & Schooler, C. (1978). The structure of coping. *Journal of Health and Social Behavior, 19,* 2–21.

Potorski, T. L. (1992). *Worksite health promotion: Rationale for military implementation.* Association of Military Surgeons of U.S., 426–430.

Selye, H. (1980). *Selye's guide to stress research.* New York: Van Nostrand.

Smerglia, V. L., Deimling, C. T., & Barresi, C. M. (1988). Black/white comparisons in helping and decision-making networks of impaired elderly. *Family Relations, 37,* 305–309.

Smith, T. W., Allred, K. D., Morrison, C. A., & Carlson, S. D. (1989). Cardiovascular reactivity and interpersonal influence: Active coping in a social context. (Abstract) *Journal of Personality and Social Psychology, 56* (2), 209–218.

Spiegel, D., & Wissler, T. (1983). Perceptions of family environment among psychiatric patients and their wives. *Family Process, 22,* 537–548.

Staples, R., & Johnson, L. (1993). *Black families at the crossroads.* San Francisco, CA: Jossey-Bass.

Staples, R. (1975): *The black family: Essays and studies.* (3rd ed.) California: Wadsworth.

Strauss, A., & Corbin, J. (1990) *Basics of qualitative research.* Newbury Park, CA: Sage.

Tomlinson, P. S. (1986). Applying family stress theory to nursing practice. *Nursing Research, 11,* 78–81.

Tucker-Allen, S. (1991). Health care in the black community. *ABNF Journal, (2)1,* 3.

Wilheim, M. S., & Ridley, C. A. (1988). Stress and unemployment in rural nonfarm couples: A study of hardships and coping resources. *Family Relations, 37,* 50–54.

Wilner, N., & Horowitz, M. (1980). Life events, stress, and coping. In Leonard W. Poon (Ed.), *Aging in the 1980's: Psychological issues.* Washington, DC: American Psychological Association.

Wilson, M. N. (1986). The black extended family: An analytical consideration. *Developmental Psychology, 22,* 246–258.

Woods, N. F., Most, A., & Longemecker, G. D. (1985). Major life events daily stressors and symptoms. *Nursing Research, 24,* 263–267.

Wright, L. M., & Leahy, M. (1984). *Nurses and families: A guide to family assessment and intervention.* Philadelphia: F.A. Davis.

Chapter Seven

Aging, Caregiving Effects, and Black Family Caregivers

Sandra Sayles-Cross

The measure of the greatness of a country is determined by:
its treatment of its underprivileged,
its treatment of its children,
its treatment of its aged.

Hubert Humphrey

One hot summer afternoon in August, 1985, the afternoon soap operas were interrupted by a news special. The body of an "elderly" woman had been discovered in the apartment she shared with her son. While the common living areas and the son's bedroom were immaculate, the mother had been living in utter filth and human excrement in her tiny room. As the story unraveled for several weeks on the nightly news, we learned that the mother had died of starvation and malnutrition. We also learned that state law did not require a child to care for a parent, even when they reside together. In a futile attempt to identify charges on which to prosecute the son, the law enforcement agencies checked all previous Internal Revenue Service records to determine if the mother had ever been claimed as a dependent by her son. She had not. So with much less fanfare, three weeks later the story disappeared from the evening news.

There is no doubt that this story is horrifying because it is contrary to commonly held American cultural values. It was especially shocking for me because this story concerned an African American family. Cultural traditions have always supported caregiving for elder family members. But this 30-second news story changed my perspective, raising numerous questions as to how basic family values may be changing. Certainly other changes in society, such as technology, dual income families, and increased life expectancy are influencing our lives. The story also stimulated my interest in learning more about elder mistreatment, ultimately the caregiving experience in America, and the perceptions of caregivers about their caregiving role.

AGING IN AMERICA

The face of America is changing. Each day we are becoming an older society with an increasing population of ethnic minorities, especially African American female elders. Black elders are the fastest growing group in the nation. By the year 2030, we can expect to have 7.3 million black elders in the United States (Sayles-Cross, 1990). No place is this changing picture more evident than in the comparison of the data from the 1980 and 1990 census reports.

Since 1980, the U.S. Department of Commerce Census Bureau (1982, 1992) has revised the age categories, adding a category for adults age 105 years and over. Furthermore, the median age of the population has increased by 2.9 years to 32.9. Females 60 years of age and older out number males in all age categories. At age 84, the number of women is more than double the number of men. Between the ages of 90 to 104, the ratio of women to men is approximately 3 to 1. Men begin to approach parity again at the age of 105 years.

Similar patterns are found for black elders. The median age for blacks though is six years less than whites and 4.8 years less than all groups. Longevity for women, however, begins two years earlier (82 years). As has been reported, black men who live beyond age 75 have good life expectancies as demonstrated by the fact that the 3 to 1 ratio of women to men is not achieved until age 94 to 104, five years later than for all adults. While elders are the fastest growing segment of our population, black women have the longest life expectancy of all groups.

Lifestyle influences longevity. The data also indicate that blacks have lifelong disadvantages, as evidenced by lower economic status, less education, substandard housing stock, and poorer health status. In contrast, research has also documented strengths in the black family. Blacks have a strong family value system. Blacks are more likely to be an integral part of the family structure, receive support from family, and be viewed positively by younger blacks. In addition, blacks have a high affiliation and belief in religion. The church is available as and is used as a support system for daily life and during moments of crisis (Sayles-Cross, 1990).

In a recent presentation I queried the audience, all employed in aging services, why they were attending a session on caregiving for black elders. A young Caucasian nursing student responded that she was there to better understanding the value system which resulted in the loving care given to black elders by young and adult family members in homes where she is a home health aid. She related that this was not her own cultural experience. Others in attendance confirmed her observations. In the subsequent session, additional social service professionals further supported her experiences. They all worked with caregiving families in rural and urban communities. They also recognized that the majority of black elder adults continue to live in the community, and do so with and because of the support and assistance of their family members.

Caregiving for elder family members is growing. This trend is expected to continue well into the next century. Given the aging of the baby boom generation of the 1950s and 1960s, which was followed by a period of zero population growth and the general trend of families having fewer children than their parents, there will be fewer children to provide care assistance. How will a growing population of black female elders, who will need assistance with daily living and management of health problems, influence the family support network, the treatment of the aged, and the profile of caregiving?

Much noteworthy research has been written on caregiving. In general, caregiving is reported to have negative effects on the physical and financial health of the caregiver and to result in intergenerational conflict. The emotional strain associated with caregiving leads to an increased use of tranquilizers and sedatives by caregivers. Caregiving also leads to caregivers restricting their personal and social lives, and may result in strained family relationships (Sayles-Cross, 1993).

Little has been written about the caregiving experience of black families. In a research review of family caregivers of chronically ill African American elders, Hines-Martin (1992) concluded that information is strikingly lacking. In a 1994 study, Price focused upon attitudes about caregiving to an elder parent in 100 mother-daughter dyads in a large metropolitan area. She found these African American daughters to have a strong sense of filial responsibility, which made them less receptive to the use of formal services. Price concluded that these caregivers were accepting of a dependent elder parent. The study documented that some caregivers hold positive attitudes about parent caring. In another 1994 study, Kelly similarly found a strong sense of filial obligation and intergenerational ties among caregivers caring for elders with dementia. African American families cling to values of responsibility to family, the extended family network, and home care for relatives for as long as feasible. However, although the available literature is growing, even less information is available on the perceptions of the effects of caregiving on black caregivers' health.

A search of the literature published between 1990 and 1994 identified only three articles published on caregiver health or well being. Two studies were written by the same researcher, M. M. Neundorfer. In 1991, Neundorfer concluded, in support of other research, that literature reports of deterioration in caregivers' physical health were exaggerated. The data, however, suggested that caregiving most affects the emotional health of caregivers. Certainly, with such apparent contradictions, the need is clear: More research is needed on the black caregiving experience for health and social service professionals to adequately assist them with this growing population.

RESEARCH PERSPECTIVE

Sayles-Cross (1993) conducted a research study of 139 family care-givers of adults 60 years of age or older. Fifty caregivers of black elders comprised a subset of this population. The data from this group were analyzed to determine the perceptions of affects of caregiving on the physical health and the emotional responses of caregivers. The data were further analyzed to identify the number and types of caregiving tasks performed. Finally, the data were analyzed to identify the demographic characteristics of the caregivers and the elder care recipients.

In this study, the caregivers were overwhelmingly female. Caregivers were principally the daughter of the elder, though four were daughters-in-law. The second largest group receiving care, however, in contrast to other reports, were aunts/uncles, more than in-laws. There were two male caregivers and only one spouse (wife) care-giver in the group. Fourteen percent (n = 7) of the caregivers were 60 years of age or older and by virtue of their age could qualify as care recipients for the purposes of this study. Unfortunately, specific data were not collected to determine the pre-existing health status or caregiving needs of the caregivers.

The care recipients were also primarily female. The eleven male care recipients were long livers. The nine males, for whom ages were reported, were equally divided among the decades of the 1970s, 1980s, and 1990s. The largest proportion of care recipients resided in the same household as the caregivers and had been receiving care assistance for more than two years (56%). Other demographic data on caregivers and care recipients are reported in Tables 1 and 2. The data suggests that aging and caregiving in this African American population was a female issue.

In this population, and as reported in other studies, caregiving activities consisted primarily of more instrumental tasks: providing transportation, handling business affairs, and writing checks to pay

Table 1
Characteristics of Caregivers and Elders

Characteristics	Caregivers	Elders
Female	96%	78%
Age range	21–68	60–96
Married/widow	54%/4%	28%/64%
Live with elder	56%	
Provide support	40%	58%
Full-time employed	64%	
College degree*	54%	

*Earned at least a bachelors degree.

bills. Activities of daily living (ADL) most frequently performed (grooming, bathing, dressing, and feeding) suggested limitations in dexterity of the care recipients. Fewer elders were reported to have difficulty with mobility and safety, requiring assistance with ambulating, toileting, or positioning in bed.

The profile of caregiving families in this study is consistent with the literature on caregivers and African American families. The

Table 2
Caregiving Activities

Activity	Frequency	Percent
Providing transportation	40	80
Managing business affairs	36	72
Grooming	31	62
Writing checks to pay bill	27	54
Bathing	24	48
Dressing	24	48
Eating/feeding	19	38
Special treatments	17	34
Ambulating	12	24
Toileting	11	22
Turning in bed	10	20

majority of elders lived with and were primarily cared for by family members. The cultural values of these families supported family care as opposed to institutional placement. Forty percent of families provided financial support to elders in addition to assisting with instrumental tasks and ADL. A significant portion of caregivers were caring for aunts/uncles supportive of strong family values which extend to relatives outside of the immediate family.

Perceptions of caregivers of the effects of caregiving on their health and emotions were analyzed with descriptive statistics. Individual emotion and health-related items were drawn from the Cost of Caring Index (Kosbert & Cairl, 1986), the Emotions Scales (Folkman & Lazarus, 1986), and the Stakes Scale (Folkman et al., 1986).

Only one of the thirteen Stakes items queried the caregiver on their concern for their own health. In one item, the caregiver was asked to rate on a five-point Likert scale their response to the statement: "In this situation there is the possibility of harm to your own health, safety, or physical well-being." Caregivers' responses were divergent; half responded that the statement did not apply to their caregiving situation while 30 and 20 percent, respectively, responded that the statement applied little/somewhat or a lot/great deal. Recognizing the potential for threats to health allows caregivers to adapt caregiving activities, implement preventive strategies, and to seek additional support from family and professionals. Unfortunately, caregivers' health is only superficially evaluated by health professionals unless the caregiver is the identified patient. A focus on providing care to the dyad, specifically the health status and needs of caregivers, can no longer be absent from our treatment plan.

Kosbert and Cairl (1986) incorporated a subscale on health implications of caregiving in their index. Four items (rated as strongly disagree, disagree, agree, and strongly agree) allowed for obtaining data of caregiving affects on health, as seen in Table 3. Overall, caregivers did not agree that caregiving was/would negatively affect their health, appetite, or level of anxiety. They did, however, perceive that they were physically fatigued as a result of caregiving. Reports of physical fatigue are commonly found in the literature

Table 3
Cost of Caring

Item Number	Question:	Disagree (%)	Agree (%)	Strongly Agree (%)
	I feel that caring for my elderly relative:			
03	has/will negatively affect my/family's physical health.	68	24	08
08	has/will negatively affect my appetite.	84	04	12
14	has/will cause me to be physically fatigued.	42	48	10
18	has/will cause me to become anxious.	64	26	10

on caregiving. As a stressor, prolonged fatigue can have considerable impact on the caregiver.

Stress is a known contributor to many health problems. Negative emotions suggest stress. Caregivers certainly experience stress in their caregiving roles. In the results of the larger study (Sayles-Cross, 1993), disgust/anger emerged as the predictor in the perceived cost of caring. Therefore, the negative emotions scale (Table 4) was incorporated into this study to determine if these emotions were prevalent in the experiences of black caregivers. As seen in Table 4, disgust/anger did not appear as significant emotions in caregiving. Moreover, none of the emotions suggested a strong emotional response in the experiences of these caregivers. In part,

Table 4

Negative Emotional Responses

Emotion	Not Apply		Little/Some		Lot/Great	
	N	%	N	%	N	%
Disgusted	29	58	15	30	06	12
Angry	29	58	15	30	06	12
Frustrated	12	24	20	40	18	36
Disappointed	19	38	12	24	09	18
Worried	05	10	21	42	24	48
Fearful	17	34	14	28	19	38
Anxious	12	24	22	44	16	32

this lack of negative emotions is captured in the words of a 28-year-old granddaughter who wrote:

> You must have a great deal of patience when being a caregiver. You have to give a little and take a little. To me it's a loving experience to care for someone who spent a third of their life caring for me, when I know myself it wasn't easy. Look at the condition one would be if we didn't give a care.

In comparing the responses of caregivers on their perceptions of their state of anxiety, differences are noted in their responses between the Emotions Scale and the Cost of Care Index. While on the Cost of Care Index, 64 percent of caregivers responded that they did not feel that caring for their elderly relative had/would cause them to become anxious, on the emotional response scale 44 percent and 32 percent, respectively, indicated they were currently experiencing a little/some, or a lot/great deal of anxiety in the caregiving experience. Anxiety is a complex phenomenon, and the discrepancy noted here suggests a need for further evaluation of anxiety in caregivers and its overall effects on caregiving.

Many studies have reported not only that caregiving is stressful for the caregiver, but that the caregiver's health may deteriorate during the caregiving process. Caregivers report not having the time to care for themselves. This lack of self-care is seen in caregivers with chronic health problems and caregivers who may be elder adults experiencing the normal changes of aging. These findings were only weakly supported in this study.

THE FUTURE OF CAREGIVING IN AFRICAN AMERICAN FAMILIES

Given the small sample size of the study and the paucity of literature on the black caregiving experience, only crystal ball gazing is practical in looking to the future. If these caregivers mirror society, however, than what we know from population projections, gerontology, and health care suggest some trends worth considering. Foremost, the longevity of the African American female and the shorter life expectancy of the African American male make the aging of the American society a vital issue in our community. What then can we expect?

We can expect an increasing number of African American females living well into old age, including their centennial years. Many of them will live alone in the community. The ability of female elders to live independently, in part, will be possible because of strong family support, especially in the provision of transportation, and the management of financial and business affairs. In spite of the dual-income nuclear family structure, caring for family members, regardless of where they reside, continues to be an important value of the African American family.

Unlike child care, caring for elder family members has no future expectations of the elder leaving the nest and becoming independent. Therefore, women will reach their golden years after long-term care of children, parents, spouses, and other relatives. The caregivers in the study reported here told of caring for parents and other family members, maintaining full-time employment, performing multiple caregiving activities, and a lengthy caregiving experience. They also reported physical fatigue as a result of caregiving.

There can be detrimental effects from performing multiple roles for extended periods. As reported, blacks traditionally have a low use of formal services. Even in the present changing environment, family assistance continues as the primary support system. Furthermore, as suggested by Bell and Femea (1993), black elder females view their health status less positively than black elder males, are more accepting of the sick role, and have a less positive health outlook. Thus, aging caregivers may find their own health status critically compromised after years of neglect. This is exemplified in the experiences of caregivers who "do not have time to recuperate after surgery" or who move from "caring first for my father and now my mother" while, at the same time, ignoring their own health and psychological needs. Professionals, of course, will be doubly challenged to increase the uses of formal services by the African American community when state and federal fiscal outlays for those services are decreasing.

These predictions suggest a need for new support services to manage instrumental tasks along with traditional personal care assistance. It further suggests the need for prevention focused self-care practices to ensure more prosperous caregiving years, and healthier golden years for females, which will delay our need for caregiving.

CONCLUSION

America is rapidly becoming an older society with an increasing number of elder black females. A parallel trend here is the growth of family caregiving. Black females are emerging as the group who are both providing care and who are the recipients of caregiving services. Cultural norms in African American families have traditionally valued caring for family members. This study suggests that these values continue in spite of the nuclear family structure, dual income families, and the known detrimental psychosocial pressures exerted on the family.

African American elders are primarily receiving care from relatives in the home, with a low use of professional services. Their support from family and their need for instrumental care assistance offers challenges for professionals in developing new formal services and creative approaches to encourage black caregiving families to use these services.

America must soon address aging as both a female and a minority issue. Aging and caregiving are truly issues for black females. We live longer than other groups, which extends our years in the caring role. We move from caring for children, to being sandwiched between kids and parents, to caring for spouses, parents, and ourselves. With the graying of society and the rising incidence of elder caregiving, America is on the horizon of measuring the greatness of itself, its people, and its future.

REFERENCES

Bell, C. E., & Femea, P. L. (1993). A comparative analysis of the health beliefs of older black males and females. *The ABNF Journal, 4*(3), 66–69.

Folkman, S., & Lazarus, R. S. (1986). Stress processes and depressive symptomatology. *Journal of Abnormal Psychology, 95*(2), 107–113.

Folkman, S., Lazarus, R. S., Dunkel-Schetter, C., DeLongis, A., & Gruen, R. J. (1986). Dynamics of a stressful encounter: Cognitive appraisal, coping and encounter outcomes. *Journal of Personality and Social Psychology, 50*(5), 992–1003.

Hines-Martin, M. P. (1992). A research review: Family caregivers of chronically ill African-American elderly. *Journal of Gerontological Nursing, 18*(2), 25–29.

Kelley, J. D. (1994). African American caregivers: Perceptions of the caregiving situation and factors influencing the delay of the institutionalization of elders with dementia. *The ABNF Journal, 5*(4), 106–109.

Kosberg, J. I., & Cairl, R. E. (1986). The cost of care index: A case management tool for screening informal care providers. *The Gerontologist, 26*(3), 273–278.

Neundorfer, M. M. (1991). Coping and health outcomes in spouse caregivers of persons with dementia. *Nursing Research, 40*(5), 260–266.

Neundorfer, M. M. (1991). Family caregivers of the frail elderly: Impact of caregiving on their health and implications for interventions. *Family Community Health, 14*(2), 48–58.

Price, M. (1994). African American daughters attitudes about caregiving to frail, elderly parents. *The ABNF Journal, 5*(4), 112–116.

Sayles-Cross, S. (1990). Perspectives on the status of elder blacks in America. *The ABNF Journal, 1*(1), 10–13.

Sayles-Cross, S. (1993). Perceptions of familial caregivers of elder adults. *Image, 25*(2), 88–92.

U.S. Department of Commerce, Census Bureau. (1982). *1980 Census of population, general population characteristics, United States.* Washington, DC: U.S. Government Printing Office.

U.S. Department of Commerce, Census Bureau. (1992). *1990 Census of population, general population characteristics, United States.* Washington, DC: U.S. Government Printing Office.

Chapter Eight

Epidemiological Findings in Understanding Mental Illness in Ethnic Minorities: The Case of Schizophrenia

Delroy M. Louden

The application of epidemiological methods to the study of psychiatric disorders is by now well established. Early focus of attention was directed at institutional populations, where the statistics of time, place, and person could be readily collected. It became immediately apparent that the quality of these data suffered from contamination by the many nosocomial factors bearing on admission to a hospital.

Historically, the central hypothesis of epidemiolocal work on migration implied that the cultural background of particular immigrant groups determines to a large extent the nature of the adaptive mechanisms evolved by each group to overcome the stresses and problems of urbanization. The extent to which adjustment is required, however, is a function of the immigrant background— urban, rural, available social network, family constellation, and the reception in the receiving society.

More recently, there has been a shift of interest directed at attempts to identify psychiatric illness in particular migrant populations. While demographic information renders such samples representative, these investigations have still to overcome the awkward problems posed by definition of caseness, that is, what constitutes a case and/or morbidity. Moreover, despite the development of more vigorous methodological techniques designed to measure psychopathology in these populations, much of the resulting material bears more upon the reliability and validity of instruments designed to apply to these communities. Despite the widespread acceptance of a role for sociocultural factors in the presentation of schizophrenia, their precise role, if any, in modifying the onset and evolution of schizophrenic symptoms remain unclear.

Cross-cultural research in symptomatology, case definition, and nosology of psychiatric disorders has traditionally been interpreted in one of two ways. The first may be characterized as the cultural-general (ethic) approach which typifies psychopathology as a universal phenomenon with sociocultural influences as mainly pathoplastic. The second may be characterized as the culture-specific (epic) approach, emphasizing differences in psychopathology between different cultures.

Torrey (1987) has also pointed out that, in the history of epidemiology, authors reporting variations in rates of schizophrenia have enthusiastically recruited their findings to support their favored theory of causation.

PREVIOUS STUDIES OF SCHIZOPHRENIA AMONG AFRO-CARIBBEAN PEOPLE

Prior to 1980, there was a dearth of studies reporting on the pattern of psychological disturbance in this population. However, since 1980 (see Table 1), interest has dramatically increased. Table 1 illustrates 12 investigations reporting an increased rate of schizophrenia among first and second generation Afro-Caribbean immigrants to the United Kingdom. Investigations such as that conducted by Cochrane and Bal (1987) have not produced the kind of consistency in their findings as throughout the Afro-Caribbean population. In a later paper examining the ethnic density hypothesis—that is, there exits an inverse relationship between the size of ethnic groups and their admission rates for psychological disorders—Cochrane and Bal reported little reason to support this hypothesis for all foreign born groups in the United Kingdom. In fact, their finding in some cases showed a significant positive relationship

Table 1

Investigations on the Rates of Illness in Patients of Afro-Caribbean Background

Author	Data Service	Diagnosis Group	Migrant Group Afro-Caribbean	English	Asian
Carpenter & Brockington (1980)	Inpatients case notes	First admission rates	*		*
		Schizophrenia	*		*
		Neuroses			*
		Personality disorder			*
Bebbington et al. (1981)	Case register	Schizophrenia	*		
		Mania	*		
Dean et al. (1981)	Hospital admissions (national)	Schizophrenia	*		
Cochrane & Bal (1987)	Hospital admissions (national)	Schizophrenia & Paranoia	*	*	
Glover (1989b)	Hospital admissions (national)	Schizophrenia	*		*
Wessley et al. (1991)	Case register	Schizophrenia	*		
Pipe et al.* (1991)	Case register	Personality disorder schizophrenia	*		
Thomas et al. (1993)	Hospital admission/readmission	Schizophrenia manic depression	*		*
Harrison et al. (1988)	Case register	Schizophrenia mania	*		
McGovern et al. (1987)	Hospital admissions	Schizophrenia cannabis psychosis	*		
Williams et al. (1990)	Case register	Functional psychoses	*		
Sugarman et al. (1992)	Central case register	Schizophrenia	*		

*Note: Reported excess for specified diagnostic groups.

between group size and admission rates. Attempts to explain the higher rates of admission of the foreign born for schizophrenia have been examined in detail. Cochrane and Bal (1987) concluded that some of the differences between the foreign born and the native born were reduced after age/sex standardization, as in the case of the Indian born of both sexes and/or Afro-Caribbean born men and women. However, a tentative explanation points toward a combination of their stressful post-migration experiences and a possible tendency to misdiagnose schizophrenia altogether in this group with respect to the differences found.

Glover (1989) examined the patterns of psychiatric admissions among Afro-Caribbean born immigrants in London and showed that for ages 15–24 and 25–34 there was an excess of admissions (p < 0.001) for schizophrenia among men. For Afro-Caribbean women, the sharp excess is confined to the youngest group. The proportion of admissions which were first admissions were significantly lower for Afro-Caribbean born from the two youngest groups of men and the three youngest groups of women, ages 15–24, 25–34, 35–44. For Afro-Caribbean women, the relative risk of all admissions was fairly steady except for the youngest group while the relative risk of first admission was inconsistent. For Afro-Caribbean men, a sharp cohort pattern was seen for all psychotic diagnoses, a fact that is equally disconcerting.

In their case control study of schizophrenia among Afro-Caribbean migrants, Wessley et al. (1991) sought to ensure that their sample met both International Classification of Disease-9 (ICD-9) codes for schizophrenia and also Research Diagnostic Criteria (RDC) or DSM-III-R criteria. Their data support previous findings of a substantial elevation in the rise of schizophrenia in second generation Afro-Caribbean born people. This study avoids some of the methodological problems that have affected other studies. Uniform criteria minimize the effect of changing diagnostic habits over time. Using incident cases eliminates duration bias; matching for age, sex, and period controls for changes in the age or gender structure of the population.

SECOND GENERATION IMMIGRANTS FROM THE CARIBBEAN IN THE UNITED KINGDOM

As used in most investigations, the definition for "second generation" is broad, including both British born Afro-Caribbeans and those who immigrated to Britain as children. Utilizing admission rates, McGovern and Cope (1987) in a retrospective study from a defined catchment area in the Midlands, England, found second generation rates raised for all diagnostic categories. Rates for second generation Afro-Caribbean males with cannabis psychosis, for example, massively exceeds that for young whites, just as rates for schizophrenia were much higher in both second generation Afro-Caribbean males and females, and especially in the latter. As to first generation Afro-Caribbeans, the rate for schizophrenia/paranoid psychosis exceeds the white rate for both sexes, but here the excess is less than that found in the second generation. In all other diagnostic groups, the white rates exceed those of the first generation Afro-Caribbean.

Age-corrected rates of schizophrenia and paranoid syndromes were approximately four times those found among non-Caribbean populations. With respect to British born Afro-Caribbean people, the size of the difference was nearly seven-fold among men and fourteen-fold among women. These statistics imply that, in normal practice, British psychiatrists are rather unwilling or unable to understand the multifaceted presentations seen in these populations and largely lump them into easily identifiable categories.

In a retrospective investigation examining psychiatric morbidity among U.K. born European, Afro-Caribbeans, and Asians within three age bands over four years, Thomas et al. (1993) found first admission rates for schizophrenia to be 320 per 100,000 population per year (95% confidence intervals 152–589). Rates of first admission of first generation Afro-Caribbeans aged 16–29 and 30–44 were significantly lower than those of age-matched Europeans (95% confidence intervals non-overlapping) ($P < 0.05$); that is, certain associations exist and are not explained by chance variations. Second-generation Afro-Caribbeans had a significantly higher rate of first admission compared with Europeans of the same age band. This was largely attributable to diagnoses of psychosis, with 10 (45%) of the second-generation Afro-Caribbean group suffering from schizophrenia and 5 (23%) from "other psychoses." The rates were nine times higher for schizophrenia and five times higher for "other psychoses" than the respective rates for age-matched Europeans. Evidently, the discrete entities for these categories are less satisfactory as evidenced by "other psychoses," a group which clearly includes cases of an organic nature.

Readmissions were significantly higher among second-generation Afro-Caribbeans (16–29) and in first-generation Afro-Caribbeans (over 30 years) when compared with age-matched Europeans.

This investigation was the first to compare rates among the British-born two major ethnic groups, namely Asians and Afro-Caribbeans. In reporting the findings, the authors caution in interpretation as the numbers of subjects within stratified ethnic groups were small and there were difficulties in estimating the various population denominators from census data. First, there was an indirect estimate of second-generation ethnic groups from "head of household" statistics. Second, the study was performed on admissions three-to-six years after the 1981 census, during which time the age structure of the ethnic group populations would have changed. The four-year study interval also meant that subjects up to four years younger than a particular age band at the beginning of the study, or up to four years older than a particular age band at the end of the study, could be considered within that age band at some stage during the study. However, even when the age structure of the 16–29 year second-generation Afro-Caribbean was increased by 59 percent as estimated for 1986, the rate of schizophrenia in this group remains five times higher than in age-matched Europeans. Had an age cohort been employed, it would have helped to establish how many subjects from which groups moved in and out of the central area during the study.

In an intriguing paper entitled, "Are British Psychiatrists Racist?" Lewis (1990) attempted to address the issue of the preponderance of schizophrenia found in Afro-Caribbean patients by looking at the issue of diagnostic bias; that is, the tendency to label immigrants with the more serious diagnostic cases of psychoses compared to less serious neurotic conditions. To test for diagnostic bias, he varied the ethnic group of patients in an otherwise identical series of case vignettes sent to a sample of British psychiatrists (N = 139). Apparently, respondents tended to under-diagnose schizophrenia in patients identified as Afro-Caribbean compared with white patients, representing a bias in the opposite direction to that initially suspected. The result supported the notion that race of the patient influences clinical predictions and attitudes of practicing psychiatrists.

The evidence also indicates that second generation Afro-Caribbean immigrants may be at much greater risk of psychiatric hospitalization or morbidity than their parents. Here, early childhood, as experienced in England, is a key psychiatric risk factor for the present generation of young Afro-Caribbeans, who are living in a society that discriminates against them and which they did not choose to live in. The combined elements of this experience may be emotional, sociological, or biological and are reviewed at length by McGovern and Cope (1987). Particularly noteworthy in their study were the sex differences observed; that is, for black males to have schizophrenia as a label applied to them more than for black females.

If, as these studies suggest, the high peak of admissions in young men is largely attributable to schizophrenia, this may explain the sex difference. This disease tends to appear about ten years earlier in men. Biological explanations involving exposure to some type for risk in early childhood would thus postulate that, in a migrating cohort exposed in their country of settlement to a risk not found in their country of origin, elevated rates of illness would appear earlier in men than women.

Littlewood (1988) also noted that the diagnosis of cannabis psychosis, for example, is applied more frequently in the Afro-

Caribbean population despite the lack of convincing evidence supporting a major ethnological role for cannabis in severe psychosis (Onyango, 1986).

In accounting for lower rates of schizophrenia as seen in Jamaica (country of origin) compared to rates seen in Afro-Caribbeans in the United Kingdom (adopted country), Hickling (1991) suggests that "higher rate has to be explained by factors operating within the countries to which they migrated, as they are much higher than admission rates in their country of origin." In other words, there are certain structural features (e.g., racism) operating in European and North American societies that are taking a heavy toll on our people.

In their review of migration and mental health among the peoples of the Caribbean, 1948–80 Thomas and Lindenthal (1989) observed:

> We find very little consideration of the culture from which West Indians migrated, nor do we gain much information about the culture and levels of tolerance among the societies to which the West Indians have migrated. It is taken for granted that readers are familiar with the latter. Data concerning the economic and political conditions motivating people to migrate are more common. On the other hand, the role of personality type, such as schizoid, in selectively motivating people to migrate has received little or no attention.
>
> Almost all studies concerning Caribbean migrants have reported high rates of schizophrenia. Although we do not quarrel with these findings generally, we think it necessary to note that one factor that may contribute to inflated false-positive rates of mental illness, particularly of schizophrenia, is the culture of the country of origin. The content and ritual of the religious systems of many of the Caribbean peoples can easily be mistaken for schizophrenic-like behavior. Under certain conditions, such as stress (and immigration certainly qualifies as a stressor), the previously learned behavior can be evoked. The validity of many diagnoses reported in the literature is founded on the assumption that true schizophrenic behavior other than the above-learned behavior was observed by the psychiatrist before the ultimate diagnosis was made.

Another related problem derives from the relatively alien and most often urban cultures to which many of the Caribbean people tend to migrate. Unfamiliar surroundings involving strange languages, customs, and modes of behavior are conducive to feelings of loneliness, isolation, and persecution on the part of the migrant. Such feelings are associated with clinical diagnoses of mental impairment, more specifically, schizophrenia.

Remarkably, 35 years earlier, Eitinger (1959), investigating the incidence of mental illness among refugees in Norway, echoed a similar view to that above when he observed that:

The first and immediate feeling in a strange milieu will usually be this particular feeling of loneliness and rejection. The manifold external expressions do not create any feelings of solidarity, of an understanding of the situation or the inner meaning of the impressions, and first and foremost, no understanding of the individual's position in the whole of this unknown and overwhelming system. It is precisely this lack of ability to receive, to understand, to develop and to react to the surroundings which causes this apparent but nonetheless very familiar paradox of feeling isolated, of being totally alone, [like] Lilly's experimental person in the water-tank, while one is actually surrounded by masses of talking, laughing, active fellow-beings, be it on Karl Johan Street in Oslo, in Piccadilly Circus in London, or on Fifth Avenue, New York. We have thus two different mechanisms which cause psychotic reactions. The primitive, unobserved feeling of being overwhelmed by outside impressions and stimuli which cannot be digested, and thus lead to confusion, and, in addition to this, the reaction to the feeling for loneliness, which is first and foremost marked by insecurity. The feeling of "not belonging"; of not being able to take a role in some form or other, of not knowing what is expected of one, adds insecurity to isolation.

Here, the most frequently asked questions by investigators involve the strength of migrant premorbid personality and variation in rates of illness from countries of origin.

Delroy M. Louden

Caribbean Regional Differences

Using population data, Glover (1989) examined the observation reported by Littlewood and Lipsedge (1982) that migrants from Jamaica were at higher risks with illnesses diagnosed as schizophrenia. Combining the number of psychiatric admission, average admission rate, and diagnostic profile of psychiatric admissions for the period 1982–1985 for Caribbean migrants living in the North West and North East regions of London showed that Jamaicans had the highest crude admission rates for both sexes by about 50 percent—a finding highly significant ($P < 0.0001$). Age-specific rates could not be calculated as the population age structure was not available for the separate islands. However, if the age "structure of the whole Caribbean born population of Greater London were mirrored in each of the island groups studies, then young (age 15–24) Jamaican and Barbarian men would experience the highest admission rates and these would drop steadily with age." That pattern could also be seen, though less sharply, for Jamaican women. Trinidadians showed much less variation across the age range (a pattern more similar to native Britons). Admission/readmission rates did not differ markedly between the three island groups.

When a comparison was made of diagnostic profile of patients from the three islands, Jamaican and Barbarian men had similar diagnostic patterns, but among Trinidadian men patients a smaller proportion received a diagnosis of schizophrenia and a larger proportion a diagnosis of mania. Among female patients, no significant differences in diagnostic pattern were seen. It is important to remember that these figures relate to number of hospital admissions and thus are subjected to all the systematic biases associated with such data.

Important among the possible explanation for the differences observed would be the variation in social structure of these islands. Psychiatric admission rates in the indigenous population of the United Kingdom and other countries have been shown to differ between different social classes. While no such studies have considered this question specifically for migrant populations, it seems at least plausible that similar patterns would be found.

Biological Factors in the Etiology of Schizophrenia

In examining the relationship between schizophrenia and immigration, Earles (1991) has posed an intriguing question: "Are there alternatives to the psychosocial hypotheses?" suggesting that there is growing support for causes and symptoms via biological abnormalities.

Viral and Infectious Agents. Schizophrenia has been found to be rare in populations who are remote from industrialized society, and who are thus presumably less likely to be exposed to the common infectious diseases.

The evidence for a viral etiology of schizophrenia, reviewed by King and Cooper (1989), has been researched using both direct and epidemiological methods. In answering the question—"Of what relevance is the findings from infectious disease such as, influenza, pneumonia, and diphtheria for understanding the excess of schizophrenia in second-generation Afro-Caribbean people in England?"—Wing (1989) has suggested that second-generation immigrants may be particularly at risk from intrauterine infections if they are unprotected by maternal antibodies to viruses to which the mother had not been previously exposed. He draws parallels with the increased rates of autism among the offspring of urban-born immigrants in Sweden (Gillbert et al., 1987). It is even possible that a similar cause may underlie the higher levels of severe mental handicap in the children of immigrants (Akinsola & Fryers, 1986). Clearly, impaired intrauterine immunity could not account for increased rates of schizophrenia in first-generation immigrants. King and Cooper (1989) have suggested that perinatal infection might lead to an immunological dysfunction, and that adult illness may be triggered by exposure to the same, or to a similar pathogen.

Obstetric Complications

Although the evidence is not consistent over a particular period of time, there is now reason to believe that obstetric complications are significantly associated with the subsequent development of schizophrenia. Eagles (1991) raised this issue when he asked: "Could rates of schizophrenia among West Indian immigrants be partly or wholly explicable in terms of an increased propensity of their mothers to suffer from obstetric and perinatal complications? In general terms, compared with native-born populations, immigrant women do indeed suffer higher rates of obstetric complications and have shorter durations of antenatal care" (Lumb et al., 1981). Caution should be exercised, however, in generalizing regarding the obstetric history of "immigrant" women as a homogeneous group. In the United Kingdom, a number of investigations have compared "obstetric performances" and perinatal complications of white, native born African-Caribbean and Asian women. Adding to their discussion, Griffiths et al. (1989) have stated, "Social adversity may also act as a proxy for other variables, of which plausible candidates include poor antenatal and perinatal care and infection." In addition, and as Owen et al. (1988) have shown, recent work suggests that obstetric complications are significantly associated with an increased risk of schizophrenia in offspring. In two other studies of the 1957 influenza epidemic in Britain, maternal viral infection during the second trimester of pregnancy was found as being associated with schizophrenia in offspring (O'Callaghan et al., 1991; Mednick et al., 1989).

Tuck et al. (1983) found no differences in perinatal mortality between black and white mothers, but did find black mothers to have higher rates of emergency Caesarean sections. The studies of Terry et al. (1987) and of Griffiths et al. (1989) both based on large birth cohorts in Birmingham, England, obtained very consistent findings here. Afro-Caribbean babies were two to three times more likely than European babies to be of very low birth weight (i.e., less than 1500g) (Terry et al., 1987). Both studies found that, despite these increased rates of very low birth weight, neonatal survival was actually higher among Afro-Caribbean babies. As a result of such researching, this question arises: Is it possible that an enhanced survival rate could contribute significantly to the greater risk of subsequent schizophrenia among second-generation, Afro-Caribbean immigrants, given that their European counterparts of low birth weight are more likely to be stillborn or to die in the neonatal period?

If obstetric complications are indeed an important factor in the etiology of schizophrenia in Afro-Caribbean immigrants, then these patients should show characteristics which cluster with a history of obstetric complications, that is, early age at onset and low genetic loading. There is some evidence from the findings of Harrison et al. (1989) that psychotic Afro-Caribbean patients had fewer relatives with a history of psychiatric illness than did their non-Caribbean counterparts. Overall, then, there is a great need for a substantial body of consistent findings before any credence with respect to genetic loading can be seriously entertained. In addition, and particularly for a population comprised of Caribbean peoples, the methodological and conceptual issues are quite complex and burdensome.

Discussion

A number of explanations have been advanced to account for the consistent finding of a disproportionate percentage of Afro-Caribbean patients labelled schizophrenic. The first such explanation concerns unemployment levels, which are significantly higher in Afro-Caribbean than in Asian populations. Similar findings were identified in Nottingham, England, with raised rates of unemployment and lower social class among Afro-Caribbeans when compared with non-Caribbeans (Harrison et al., 1989). These findings reflect the serious unemployment situation among Afro-Caribbean patients have led to the suggestion that they were more socially disadvantaged than European or Asian patients. Although housing did not form part of their enquiry, clinic experience confirmed Deakin's (1970) report that Afro-Caribbean patients usually lived in homes which were decaying and in a poor state of repair. The association between deprived, run-down inner-city areas and high rates of psychiatric admission is also well-documented (Faris & Dunham, 1939; Hare, 1956; Ineichen et al., 1984; Giggs & Cooper, 1987).

Misdiagnosis. It has been suggested that acute psychotic reactions may be misdiagnosed as schizophrenia (Littlewood & Lipsedge, 1981; Mukherjee et al., 1983; Cochrane & Bal, 1987).

A separate study on the same patient population reported by Thomas et al. (1993) found a high concordance rate between diagnosis of schizophrenia recorded in case notes and that arrived at by the researchers using Research Diagnostic Criteria (Stone & Osborne, 1993; Spitzer et al., 1978). Their findings were also similar to those of Harrison et al. (1988) who used the Present State Examination to measure psychiatric disorder (Wing et al., 1974). In the Harrison et al. (1989) prospective study of Afro-Caribbeans who made contact with the psychiatric service, they failed to find a higher population of patients with paranoid symptoms. Furthermore, affective symptoms were absent, thereby strengthening the argument against viewing these syndromes as misdiagnosed affective disorders.

Religion. In their investigation, Harrison et al. (1988) examined patients' current religious affiliation and any recent change in religious interest, following reports by Littlewood and Lipsedge (1981) that religious delusion constituted an important element of atypical psychoses in Afro-Caribbean patients. Their findings suggest that the emergence of religious interest changes the course of the psychosis but with surprisingly few differences between those presenting in Afro-Caribbean and other psychotic patients. When considering any increase in intensity or participation in religious activities already present, more non-Caribbean patients show changes during the course of their illness, although there are no significant differences. Interpretations of religious activities as delusive or nondelusive are fraught with difficulties. One must be mindful of not using Eurocentric world views with their inherent biases toward grouping individuals without sufficient discretion. Indeed, recent changes in the new Diagnostic and Statistical Manual-IVR (DSM-IVR), and specifically in regard to the "religious experience," point toward a recognition of this dilemma.

DRUG MISUSE AND CANNABIS

Investigations by McGovern and Copes (1987a) have suggested cannabis use as a cause of psychotic illness. On the other hand, Stone and Osborn (1993) found that there was no significant difference between the proportions of Afro-Caribbeans and Europeans who smoked cannabis in the week before admission; and in none was it considered to be etiologically responsible for the illness.

HIGHER RATES OF ILLNESS IN THE RESPECTIVE COUNTRY OF ORIGIN

Although the evidence is far from convincing, the epidemiological literature on migration and mental illness continues to promote the observation that rates of schizophrenia among migrants is often higher in their country of origin. Following such reasoning, then, the higher rates of schizophrenia found among Afro-Caribbean immigrants is simply a reflection of those to be found in their homelands. From Jamaica, in 1974, for instance, Burke found that of 41 percent of males admitted for treatment between the ages of 15–24 many suffered from schizophrenia. Regrettably, no absolute rates were calculated here. In an earlier investigation, Royes (1962) showed that first admission rates for schizophrenia in Jamaica were similar to those in the United Kingdom. Total population and annual incidence rates in these two studies were 2.7 and 1.5 per 10,000, respectively, in Jamaica. Such rates were based upon first admissions, with authors making most of the diagnoses personally, and without recourse to standardized criteria. Hickling's (1991) population-based rates for psychiatric hospital admission rates in Jamaica for 1971 through 1988 provide our most recent evidence. The overall psychiatric hospital admission rates in Jamaica were 136 per 100,000 in 1971 and 69 per 100,000 in 1988. The admission rate for schizophrenia was 69 per 100,000 in 1971 and 35 per 100,000 in 1988. This admission rate for schizophrenia is five times lower than the rate reported for Afro-Caribbeans in the United Kingdom by a number of studies, and is more in keeping with the admission rate for schizophrenia reported for the general population in England.

Propensity to Migrate among Individuals Predisposed to Schizophrenia

There are two lines of reasoning here. The first is that intermarriage among genetically predisposed first-generation immigrants often leads to even higher rates of schizophrenia among their children. With respect to Afro-Caribbean people in the United Kingdom, the findings of Thomas et al. (1993) support this view. The second refers to instability in the premorbid personality of these individuals coupled with social stress of migration, thereby precipitating a schizophrenic break.

Social Adversities and Social Stress

In 1988, Littlewood and Lipsedge suggested the existence of a psychological link between migration and schizophrenia, with the experience of migration and its aftermath causing or precipitating the illness. However, Thomas et al. (1993) argue that disorders known to be stress related, for example, neuroses, were not over represented among African American and Asians and did not show increased rates of schizophrenia. Being black, of course, is associated by the wider society with unemployment, inadequate housing, and low social class (Townsend et al., 1988), as well as wider disruptions in and impairment of family functioning (Brown, 1984). It is probable that any of these factors could directly result in a worse prognosis, and hence the higher prevalence of schizophrenia in the Afro-Caribbean population.

Racism. Burke (1984) and Littlewood et al. (1988) have argued that racial discrimination is a major contributing factor, whereas Bagley (1975) sees the unique beliefs of Afro-Caribbeans within the context of being "British"; their suffering from unfulfilled expectations of assimilation can often lead to mental illness. A similar argument, previously developed in the United States by Parker and Kliner (1961), considers goal striving and stress as causative factors. However, the Thomas et al. (1993) findings that Asians in Britain had a much *lower* rate of schizophrenia than Afro-Caribbeans suggest that the influence of racism is worthy of continued investigation. In addition, the most glaring limitation in the studies reviewed here concerns definitions of schizophrenia which are unstandardized. Further limitations involve data gathering methodology itself: Place of birth is not always recorded; ethnicity seldom recorded at interview, thereby excluding all those of Afro-Caribbean ethnically born in Britain; and there is an over reliance on hospital admissions.

Of note here is the status usually accorded to country of birth, which should not be seen as synonymous with ethnicity. Even further question marks hover over the interpretability of first admission data. On the one hand, there may be several reasons why a re-admission might be recorded as a first admission, thus inflating the first admission rate at the expense of re-admission rates. Such factors as the patient's memory, geographical mobility, and the thoroughness of information upon admission will have an influence. On the other hand, if a patient has been admitted with a particular diagnosis on previous occasions, their "first" admission with a different diagnosis will not count as such, thus depressing first admission rates for that diagnosis. The use of rates contextualizing all admissions will overcome this problem, however.

CONCLUSION

The high rates of schizophrenia attributed to Afro-Caribbean people, if they are not due to methodological error or an artifact of the system of health care delivery, do reflect an increased incidence of the disorder among this group. The overall evidence presented here demonstrates that, compared to the general population, a significantly higher proportion of Afro-Caribbeans than Asians are admitted and diagnosed with schizophrenia. Causative factors include higher rates of unemployment which suggest greater socio-economic disadvantage and reduced social cohesion in the Afro-Caribbean community. Efforts aimed at improving social disadvantages across the board, a provision for enhanced possibilities for employment, and improved mental health service delivery to such communities is overdue.

Furthermore, while it is generally accepted that the course of schizophrenia can be influenced by family and social factors, there is a general dearth of evidence that psychosocial stress or disadvantage is of primary etiological significance in schizophrenia (Hare, 1987; Leff, 1987). For example, adverse, independent life events seem to be no more common before the onset of schizophrenia than they are in control subjects (Jacobs & Myers, 1976).

Currently, multistage etiologies of increasing complexity are being brought forward to account for the phenomena and to increase our understanding of it. The excess of schizophrenia among

British Afro-Caribbean people is still a case in point. The subtle, underlying message which is not being made explicit in some investigations points toward a biological mechanism as yet poorly understood that may produce behavior which leads to an eventual diagnosis of schizophrenia. In addition, and equally important, are the effects of recognized contexts of oppression, whether through racism or family dynamics, that produce similar symptoms and can lead to a similar diagnostic outcome. Until the etiology of the condition (or conditions) is clarified, and its (or their) validity well tested, epidemiological studies remain hazardous. It is incumbent for future investigators to control carefully for possible interviewing variables such as age, social background, sex, educational status, and regional differences.

If we are to successfully relate these findings to the experiences of migrants and their psychiatric predicament, we need to provide a more broadly based measure of stressors, focussing not only on major life events. Monroe (1983) has found, for instance, that minor or daily stressors can be more predictive of changes in symptoms than major life events. In addition, and in regard to data gathering methods as well, there are limitations in the use of questionnaires or fixed interview schedules for the assessment of life stressors. This is particularly true with regard to the assessment of characteristics of life events such as threat, disruption of activity, symbolic and real loss, and so on, which require that the event be considered within the context of the individual's life circumstances.

In addition, there are a number of methodological problems to attend to; for example, biases or errors in recall or the possibility of recent symptoms influencing levels of stressors can better be dealt with through the use of longitudinal studies using repeated measures over time. Such investigation allows for the examination of the effects of stress while minimizing variability and vulnerability. The advantage of longitudinal designs, which has yet to be exploited in studying schizophrenia in migrant populations, is the opportunity that they provide for statistically controlling the influence of prior levels of symptoms in any relationship found between subsequent stressors and symptoms (Billings & Moos, 1982). Furthermore, longitudinal data are more likely to provide evidence by which to evaluate the possibility that there are identifiable subgroups of schizophrenic patients who differ to the extent to which the course of their disorder is influenced by life event stressors.

Research on life event stressors and symptoms in schizophrenia has attempted to relate variation in naturally occurring life events to differences in symptom state. There are well known limitations to correlational approaches (even if truly prospective) in allowing inferences about causal relations such as the effects of stress on symptoms. The difficulties in identifying causality are even more apparent when we consider the plausibility of, and evidence for, arguments that stress-symptom relationships are likely to be influenced by a complex set of mediating factors and processes, including various ecological, biological, psychological, and social resources (Coyne & Holroyd, 1982; Folkman et al., 1986).

Future research in this area should emphasize a number of approaches: (a) truly prospective studies of people who are vulnerable to schizophrenia, as reflected in previous episodes or clear biological vulnerability; (b) studies of the effectiveness of interventions designed to reduce life event stress. Such research should use measures which assess variables on a continuum in order to examine both major and minor life events as predictors of, and influences on, a wide spectrum of symptoms that are displayed by schizophrenic patients; and (c) investigations and comparison of rates from country of origin using standardized measures.

Quite striking from a cross-cultural psychiatric point of view is the neglect on the part of expressed emotion researchers in calling for systematic examination of the relationship between culture and expressed emotion as it applies to schizophrenia.

It can be argued that the nature of expressed emotion (in the form of verbal criticism and emotional over involvement) is clearly grounded in cultural conventions and is culture specific. However, another kind of relationship pertains here as well: Concepts such as critical comments and emotional over involvement are clearly relevant to an understanding of schizophrenia and are not necessarily ethnocentric or culture bound.

It is desirable that future investigations utilize longitudinal design with multiple interviews over at least a one-year period. This will meet several objectives which include following individuals without specific disorders at initial interview to calculate incidence rates; following those with disorders to calculate remission rates; and following those with disorders in the past to calculate recurrence rates. Furthermore, a true use of longitudinal designs will make possible detailed studies of interval service use rates.

REFERENCES

Akinsola, H. A., & Fryers, T. (1986). A comparison of patterns of disability in severely mentally handicapped children of different ethnic origins. *Psychological Medicine, 16,* 127–133.

Bissenden, J. G. et al. (1987). Ethnic differences in incidence of very low birth weight and neonatal deaths among normally formed infants. *Archives of Disease of Childhood, 62,* 709–711.

Brown, C. (1984). Black and White Britain: The PSI Survey. London: Heinemann.

Burke, A. W. (1974). First admissions and planning in Jamaica. *Social Psychiatry, 9,* 39–45.

Burke, A. W. (1984). Racism and psychological disturbance among West Indians in Britain. *International Journal of Social Psychiatry, 30,* 50–68.

Cochrane, R., & Bal, S. S. (1987). Migration and schizophrenia: An examination of five hypotheses. *International Journal of Social Psychiatry, 22,* 181–191.

Cochrane, R., & Bal, S. S. (1989). Mental hospital admission rates of immigrants to England: A comparison of 1971 and 1981. *Social Psychiatry and Psychiatric Epidemiology, 24,* 2–11.

Cooper, P., Osborn M., Gath, D. & Feggetter, G. (1982). Evaluation of a modified self-report measure of social adjustment. *British Journal of Psychiatry, 141,* 68–75.

Earles, J. M. (1991). The relationship between schizophrenia and immigration. *British Journal of Psychiatry, 159,* 783–789.

Eitinger L. (1959) The incidence of mental disease among refugees in Norway. *Journal of Mental Science, 105,* 326–380.

Faris, R. E. L., & Dunham H. W. (1939). Mental disorders in urban areas. An ecological study of schizophrenia and other psychoses. Chicago, IL: *University of Chicago Press.*

Giggs, J. A., & Cooper, J. E. (1987). Ecological structure and the distribution of schizophrenia and affective psychoses in Nottingham. *British Journal of Psychiatry, 151,* 627–633.

Gillberg, C., Steffenburg, S., Borjesson, B. et al. (1987). Infantile autism in children of immigrant parents: A population based study from Goteborg. *British Journal of Psychiatry, 150,* 856–858.

Glover, G. R. (1989). Why is there a high rate of schizophrenia in British Caribbean? *British Journal of Hospital Medicine, 42,* 48–51.

Glover, G. R. (1989b). Differences in psychiatric admission patterns between Caribbean from different islands. *Social Psychiatry and Psychiatric Epidemiology, 24,* 209–211.

Gordon, E. B. (1965). Mentally ill West Indians. *British Journal of Psychiatry, 111,* 877–887.

Griffith, R., White, M., & Stonehouse, M. (1989). Ethnic differences in birth statistics from central Birmingham. *British Medical Journal, 298,* 94–95.

Hare, E. H. (1986). Aspects of the epidemiology of schizophrenia. *British Journal of Psychiatry, 149,* 554–561.

Hare, E. H. (1987). Epidemiology of schizophrenia and affective psychoses. *British Medical Bulletin, 43,* 514–530.

Harrison, G. (1990). Searching for the causes of schizophrenia: The role of migrant studies. *Schizophrenia Bulletin, 16,* 663–671.

Harrison, G., Owens, D., Holton, A., Felton, D., & Boot, D. (1988). A prospective study of severe mental disorder in Afro-Caribbean patients. *Psychological Bulletin, 18,* 643–657.

Harrison, G., Owens, D. Holton, A., Neilson, D., Boot, D., & Cooper, J. (1989). Severe mental disorder in Afro-Caribbean patients: Some social, demographic, and service factors. *Psychological Medicine, 19,* 683–696.

Harvey, I., Williams, M., McGuffin, P., & Toone, B. K. (1990). The functional psychoses in Afro-Caribbean. *British Journal of Psychiatry, 157,* 515–522.

Hickling, F. W. (1991). Psychiatric hospital admission rates in Jamaica, 1971–1988. *British Journal of Psychiatry, 159,* 817–821.

Ineichen, B. (1989). Afro-Caribbean and the incidence of schizophrenia: A review. *New Community, 15,* 341.

King, D. J., & Cooper, S. J. (1989). Viruses, immunity, and mental disorder. *British Journal of Psychiatry, 154,* 1–7.

Lewis, G., Croft-Jeffreys, C., & David, A. (1990). Are British psychiatrists racist? *British Journal of Psychiatry, 157,* 410–415.

Littlewood, R., & Lipsedge, M. (1982) *Aliens and alienists: Ethnic minorities and psychiatry.* Hammondsworth, England: Penguin.

Littlewood, R., & Lipsedge, M. (1981). Acute psychotic reactions in Caribbean-born patients. *Psychological Medicine, 11,* 303–318.

Littlewood, R., & Lipsedge, M. (1988). Psychiatric illness among British Afro-Caribbean. *British Medical Journal, 296,* 950–951.

Littlewood, R., & Lipsedge, M. (1981a). Some social and phenomenological characteristics of psychotic immigrants. *Psychological Medicine, 11,* 289–302.

Lumb, K. M., Congdon, P. J., & Lealman, G. T. (1981). A comparative review of Asian and British born maternity patients in the United Kingdom. *British Journal of Psychiatry, 149,* 265–273.

McGovern, D., & Cope, R. (1987). First psychiatric admission rates of first and second generation Afro-Caribbean. *Social Psychiatry, 22,* 139–149.

McGovern, D., & Cope, R. V. (1987). The compulsory detention of males of different ethnic groups with special reference to offender patients. *British Journal of Psychiatry, 150,* 502–512.

Mednick, S. A., Machon, R. A., Huttanen, M. O. et al. (1988). Adult schizophrenia following prenatal exposure to an influenza epidemic. *Archives of General Psychiatry, 45,* 189–192.

Mukerjee, S., Shukla, S., Woodle, J. et al. (1983). Misdiagnosis of schizophrenia in bipolar patients: A multi-ethnic comparison. *American Journal of Psychiatry, 140,* 1571–1574.

O'Callaghan, E., Sham, P., Takei, N., Glover, G., & Murray, R. M. (1991). Schizophrenia after prenatal exposure to 1957 A2 influenza epidemic. *The Lancet, 337,* 1248–1250.

Office of Population Censuses and Surveys. (1986). The Labor Force Survey 1983 and 1984. London: Series LFS NO. 4 HMSO.

Onyango, R. S. (1986). Cannabis psychosis in young psychiatric inpatients. *British Journal of Addiction, 81,* 419–423.

Owen, M. J., Lewis, S. W., & Murray R. M. (1988). Obstetric complications and schizophrenia: A computed tomographic study. *Psychological Medicine, 18,* 331–339.

Owens, D., Harrison, G., & Boot, D. (1991). Ethnic factors in voluntary and compulsory admissions. *Psychological Medicine,* 21, 185–196.

Pipe, R., Bhat, A., Mathews, B., & Hampstead, J. (1991) Section 136 and African/Afro-Caribbean minorities. *International Journal of Social Psychiatry, 37,* 15–23.

Royes, K. (1962) The incidence and features of psychosis in a Caribbean community. In *Proceedings of the Third World Congress of Psychiatry.* Montreal: University of Toronto Press and McGill University Press.

Spitzer, R., Endicott, J., & Robins, E. (1975). *Research diagnostic criteria.* New York: New York State Psychiatric Institute.

Stone, C. W., & Osborn, M. F. (1993). A comparison of psychotic Afro-Caribbean and indigenous white patients. *Social Psychiatry.*

Sugarman, P. A. (1992). Outcome of schizophrenia in the Afro-Caribbean community. *Social Psychiatry—Psychiatry and Epidemiology, 27L,* 102–105.

Terry, P. B., Condie, R. G., & Settatree, R. S. (1980). Analysis of ethnic differences in perinatal statistics. *British Medical Journal, 281,* 1307–1308.

Thomas, G., & Lindenthal, J. (1990). Migration and mental health among the peoples of the Caribbean, 1948–1980. *Journal of Mental Health, 18,* 92–102.

Thomas, S. C., Stone, K., Osborn, M., Thomas, P. F., & Fisher, M. (1993). Psychiatric morbidity and compulsory admission among

United Kingdom born Europeans, Afro-Caribbean and Asians in Central Manchester. *British Journal of Psychiatry, 163,* 91–99.

Torrey, E. F. (1987). Prevalence studies in schizophrenia. *British Journal of Psychiatry, 150,* 598–608.

Townsend, P., Phillimore, P., & Beattie, A. (Eds). (1988). *Health and deprivation: Inequality and the North.* London: Croom Helm.

Tuck, S. M., Cardozo, L. D., Studd, J. W. W. et al. (1983). Obstetric characteristics in different racial groups. *British Journal of Obstetrics and Gynecology, 90,* 892–897.

Wessley, S., Castle, D., & Murray, G. (1991) Schizophrenia and Afro-Caribbeans. A case control study. *British Journal of Psychiatry, 159,* 795–801.

Wing, J. K. (1989). Schizophrenic psychoses: Causal factors and risks. In P. Williams, G. Wilkinson, & K. Rawnsley (Eds.), *The scope of epidemiological psychiatry.* London: Routledge.

I _ndex_

Index

Other Books of Interest from NLN Press

Book Title	Pub. No.	Price	NLN Member Price
☐ **The Path We Tread: Blacks in Nursing Worldwide, 1854–1994 (3rd ed.)** By Elizabeth Carnegie	19-2678	$30.95	$27.95
☐ **On Nursing: A Literary Celebration** By Margretta Styles & Patricia Moccia	14-2512	29.95	26.95
☐ **On Nursing: A Literary Celebration** Collector's Leatherette-Bound Edition	14-2513	54.95	49.95
☐ **Annual Review of Women's Health, Volume II** Edited by Beverly McElmurry & Randy Spreen Parker	19-2669	37.95	34.35
☐ **In Women's Experience** Edited by Patricia Munhall	14-2612	37.95	34.35
☐ **Health as Expanding Consciousness (2nd ed.)** By Margaret A. Newman	14-2626	35.95	32.35
☐ **Managing Your Career in Nursing (2nd ed.)** By Frances Henderson & Barbara McGettigan	14-2640	29.95	26.95
☐ **Nursing Centers: The Time Is Now** Edited by Barbara Murphy	41-2629	25.95	22.95